GW00786337

GOD WITH US

Family Prayer from
Advent to the Epiphany

Stuart Thomas

Kevin Mayhew

First published in Great Britain in 1991 by
KEVIN MAYHEW LTD
Rattlesden
Bury St Edmunds
Suffolk IP30 0SZ

ISBN 0 86209 193 4

Front Cover designed by Graham Johstone
Typesetting and page creation by Anne Hallam
Printed and bound in Great Britain by
J. B. Offset Printers (Marks Tey) Limited

Contents

Introduction

SOME OF US can remember when family prayers were the order of the day, but that day has now passed. Perhaps the thought of the whole family gathered around the Bible seems rather Victorian, and unduly moralistic for our present generation. As a result, many children are growing up with the assumption that family prayers are of no importance, and that any sort of personal devotions must of necessity be boring. Even in families which like the idea, the pressures of life militate against everyone coming together for even a few minutes, as members rush off to work or school, or return home at odd times. At best prayers get squeezed in between breakfast and the school bus, or between teatime and bath-time! More likely, they'll be squeezed out.

God With Us is a book of short readings from the Bible with a commentary and a prayer for each day, to last from Advent Sunday through to Epiphany. Its intention is to set Christmas in its proper context of Advent and Epiphany, so that a much wider picture can be gained of God's purposes for mankind. It's also meant to be fun, and stimulating, so that by using it the whole family can find something to awaken them spiritually. There are suggestions for ways to involve and interest younger children; for teenagers and adults there are discussion starters to pursue the issues raised. The material is intentionally flexible, and you should use it and adapt it to your own needs as a family. Clearly, younger families (those with children under 11) will probably not want to tackle the discussion starters – they're designed for teenagers and adults to get their teeth into. Likewise, if there are no First or Middle School children in your family, you might not necessarily want to do the activities intended for that age group. You could even devise your own stories to help illustrate particular points. The material has been based loosely on the alternative lectionary contained in *The Promise of His Glory*, but for the most part the readings are part of an overall theme rather than consecutive. Bible-reading and prayer are exciting and rich: children who learn to treasure them while young are more likely to hold on to them in later life. The Advent symbolism – of light, of the kingship of Jesus, of anticipation, of new and unending life – can influence all of us at a profound level, and draw us deeper into the heart of the message of Christmas-tide.

Most of all, *God With Us* has been written to enable family members of all ages to develop a living relationship with God through his Son. As we take in the themes of Advent, the familiar narrative of Christmas, and the broader perspective of Epiphany, we can experience again the wonder of God's love for us; the amazing initiative he took to restore us to living in his presence; and the reality that Emmanuel did not just come two thousand years ago – he's still 'God With Us' now, and for ever.

My thanks are due to my own family – Kathy, my wife, and Bethan, our daughter – who not only put me up to writing this, but put up with me while I did! But for them I would have no opportunity to live out the Christian faith in a family context, and their patience and love has contributed a great deal to the production of this book. I should also thank the Cleave, the Pearson and the Foulkes families, all of whom read parts of the manuscript and 'road-tested' it. Many of the ideas for activities with younger children were contributed by Christine Cleave.

Advent

ADVENT SUNDAY marks the start of the Church's new year. In Latin it means 'coming' or 'arrival', so it's a time when Christians look forward in anticipation to the coming of Jesus at Christmas. Sadly, it's become all but drowned by the torrent of parties and preparations, but traditionally it was kept as a time of penitence and fasting. Advent is to Christmas what Lent is to Easter – a time for us to prepare our own lives for the living Lord to come and dwell.

Originally Easter was the great Christian festival – the early Church preached the death and resurrection of Jesus above all else. Lent became the time for those who were to be baptised on Easter Day to prepare themselves. It seems that Christmas, the festival of Christ's birth, wasn't widely celebrated until the fourth century. Even then, the East did not accept the Western Church's date of December 25th, and instead used January 6th. Only at the beginning of the fifth century was the Western date agreed, and January 6th became the festival for the visit of the Wise Men. As Christmas grew in importance, so Advent became a time of preparation. Not surprisingly, it also became a time for remembering Jesus' promise to return to this earth in glory.

Advent has some rich and wonderful themes, which can get lost if Christmas itself starts too early. The Advent Wreath, which we consider in detail on page 9, emphasises the theme of light, and candles are a powerful reminder of Jesus, the Light of the World. But we consider too his kingship, and the way in which the prophets of the Old Testament are seen in the New to find the ultimate fulfilment of their words in Jesus Christ. It's a time for anticipation and expectation as we build up to the great festival of Christmas itself. It's a time to repent, to put our own lives right by allowing God to forgive and renew us, and to prepare ourselves spiritually to receive him as our Saviour and King.

The first week of Advent emphasises that 'getting ready' for the coming King, while the theme of the second is the link between the Old Testament and the New, focusing on the person of Jesus. The third concentrates on John the Baptist and his call to repentance, while the fourth uses Mary's openness and obedience to lead us on to the birth of Christ. That week also focuses on some of the Old Testament prophecies. Most of all Advent helps us to understand the significance of Christmas for us, here and now. The world's celebrations seem determined to keep it firmly in the past. By looking forward and entering into it, we open up our own lives to receive Jesus and acknowledge him as our king, renewing our allegiance to him. The best thing of all about Advent is that it makes Christmas so much more exciting!

Note
The calendar means that Advent varies in length. You should use as many of the weekday readings for the week of the Fourth Sunday in Advent as you need, but move on to Christmas Eve when you get there!

An Advent Prayer

To us a child is born, to us a son is given.

Wonderful Counsellor,
give your wisdom to the rulers of the nations.
Lord, in your mercy,

hear our prayer.

Mighty God, make the whole world know
that the government is on your shoulders.
Lord, in your mercy,

hear our prayer.

Everlasting Father,
establish your reign of justice and righteousness for ever.
Lord, in your mercy,

hear our prayer.

Prince of Peace,
bring in the endless Kingdom of your peace.
Lord, in your mercy,

hear our prayer.

Almighty Lord,
hear our prayer,
and fulfil your purposes in us,
as you accomplished your will
in our Lord Jesus Christ.

Amen.

The Advent Wreath

THE ADVENT WREATH is an increasingly popular symbol of the themes of Advent. As far as is known, it originated in Germany, and is sometimes called the Advent Crown (or less interestingly, the Advent Ring). It's circular in shape, representing the unending love of God, and traditionally made up of evergreen foliage. Into this ring are placed four candles, one of which is lit on Advent Sunday. Then two are lit the following Sunday, and so on until Christmas Day when a white candle, symbolising the coming of Christ, the Light of the World, is placed in the centre of the ring. As the candles are lit each Sunday a prayer is said, bringing out the theme for that week. A suggestion for these prayers is given, but you could easily make up your own. Beware of using the Advent Wreath as an early Christmas decoration – it will exercise its symbolism best as the Christian themes are brought out. That way the sense of anticipation and expectation can be built up to their climax on Christmas Day.

Shops that sell Christmas decorations may sell a ready-made Advent ring. Basically it's a candle-holder with four spaces for candles and sometimes one in the centre. Some are made of glass, so shops specialising in that sort of product might also have them for sale. These often come from Germany and can be expensive, though they'll last for many years. You can also buy small decorations for the base of the candles, but it's just as nice to use fresh foliage from the garden. If you don't want the expense of buying a ring, it's fairly simple to create one from a shallow pie dish and oasis. First, cover the dish with silver foil, then place the oasis inside it. Next, place the four red candles around the outside of the ring, equally spaced – make sure they stand upright, or they'll fall over whenever anyone jogs the table! You can then make a ring of evergreen foliage, using whatever's available at the time. Holly has a long tradition as a symbol of Christmas, but conifer and other leaves are just as good.

Do the same with a smaller piece of oasis in the middle of the dish and the Christmas candle can be placed there. You'll need to keep the oasis damp, or the leaves will soon die off, but if you overwater it, the candles may become unsteady.

Each week, at breakfast, or whenever the whole family eats together on Sunday, the appropriate number of candles are lit and the prayer for that week is said. You should let the candles burn until the end of the meal. It's an excellent idea to associate this with food, as there are many food customs in the run up to Christmas. In many European countries special cakes and biscuits are made for Advent (in Holland and Germany a tray of them is often left out for St Nicholas on December 6th). In Britain, 'Stir-up Sunday' (named after Cranmer's Collect for the Sunday before Advent), is traditionally the time for stirring the Christmas pudding mixture. Another Advent tradition is opening a special Advent calender each day. Many of these have a chocolate behind each flap, but it's also more helpful to find one which brings out the Christian themes. If Christmas starts too early the sense of anticipation is lost, and one of the richest parts of the Christian year loses its impact and identity. By exploring Advent more fully, Christmas is set in its context and understood and appreciated more fully.

Prayers for the Advent Wreath

Advent Sunday
Lord Jesus, Light of the World,
born in David's city of Bethlehem,
born like him to be a king:
be born in our hearts this Christmas-tide,
be king of our lives today.

2nd Sunday in Advent
Lord Jesus, Light of the world,
the prophets said you would bring peace
and save your people in trouble:
give peace in our hearts at Christmas-tide
and show the world God's love.

3rd Sunday in Advent
Lord Jesus, Light of the world,
John told the people to prepare,
for you were very near:
as Christmas grows closer day by day,
help us to be ready to welcome you now.

4th Sunday in Advent
Lord Jesus, Light of the world,
blessed is Gabriel who brought good news;
blessed is Mary who obeyed your will.
Bless your Church preparing for Christmas;
and bless us your children who long for your coming.

Christmas Day
Lord Jesus, Light of Light,
you have come among us.
Help us, who live by your light,
to shine as lights in your world.
Glory to God in the highest!

When you've lit the candles, say the prayer for the day together.

11

First Sunday in Advent: Get Ready!

Reading: Matthew 24:37-44

Are you looking forward to Christmas? Has anyone asked you that already? It's a difficult question to answer, because we all look forward to different things about Christmas Day. Small children get really excited at the thought of opening presents on Christmas morning – so do some rather bigger children! But they also like the idea of time off school, parties and being with friends. Grown-ups may anticipate with relish the chance to relax and sit down for a couple of days. The trouble with Christmas is that we spend a month getting ready for it, and December can seem very fraught at times. Peace and goodwill seem a long way off when we take half an hour queuing to pay for something, when we can't think of anything Uncle Jim could possibly want this year, or when we're trying to work out how we'll afford all the extra expense. We become so exhausted preparing for Christmas that by the time it arrives it feels like a big let-down.

We use up so much time and energy on organising our own enjoyment that we can't think about anything else. We forget that the decorations and Christmas dinner aren't the most important part of Christmas. Some of the people who lived at the same time as Jesus were like that. They were looking forward to the Messiah coming, but what they really wanted was someone who'd get rid of the Roman puppet government and become a great national hero. They thought the Messiah would come to restore the great days of King David's reign and bring back peace and freedom and prosperity. Because they were expecting a political figure they were totally unprepared for Jesus. When he arrived on the scene he soon became very unpopular with them.

In today's Bible reading Jesus is warning them that they must keep their eyes open if they want to see what God's doing. If they don't, they'll never be ready for it. Buying presents and sending cards are great fun, but if that's all we do, we'll be as unprepared as they were for Jesus to come to us. We can't see God at work if we don't open our eyes, or our lives, to let him come in and transform them. Advent is a time for getting ready, for preparing our own lives for King Jesus to come and change them. When he lived on earth he brought many changes, especially to those who were willing to accept him. If we're open to him and let him start to make a difference to our lives, we'll discover that we can see Christmas in a completely new light. That makes getting ready for Christmas much more exciting – something we can really look forward to!

Prayer
Lord Jesus,
we get so busy at Christmas
that we easily forget about you.
Please help us to see
what you want to do in our lives,
and to be ready for you to come
and be our King
so that we can look forward to Christmas
as a time to enjoy your presence.
Amen.

For Younger Children: Discuss what everyone in the family is most looking forward to at Christmas, and then talk about how to prepare for it. Stirring the pudding is a useful visual aid, but any food preparations or decorations will do. Emphasise the importance of being properly ready so that we can fully enjoy the big day. Start Advent with a family stir of the Christmas pudding or cake mix, if you make your own. If not, find some other practical preparation that everyone can join in (preparing a menu for Christmas, for example). Discuss what everyone in the family is most looking forward to, and how best to prepare for it. Emphasise that proper preparation is essential if we are to enjoy Christmas.

To Discuss: How can you make time for Jesus this month and get ready for Christmas in the right way?

Monday: Wake Up!

Reading: Romans 13:11-14

The trouble with waking up is that it's often easier said than done! On a chilly winter morning, while it's still dark, there's nothing better than curling up under the bedclothes and dozing off again. It's a real shock to the system when we push back the quilt, stand up, and stagger to the bathroom, shivering and rubbing our eyes. Unfortunately, if we stay in bed, the day gets lighter, time goes by, and soon we're racing round the house in a desperate struggle to get to school or work on time. We realise too late that there isn't enough time to do everything we'd planned. Then just as we're getting into our stride we realise we've put the wrong jumper on, or our socks don't match!

Paul wanted the Christians in the church at Rome to wake up. He didn't particularly want to improve their morning timekeeping, but he did want to improve their spiritual lives. He knew how easy it is to 'go to sleep' spiritually – shutting our eyes to the light that is Jesus, staying comfortable, doing nothing. But it's almost 'daytime', and nothing we do will stop it coming. If we remain asleep we'll wake up too late and realise that time and opportunity have vanished. That's why Paul stresses the importance of us taking care to put God first and not let the concerns of our everyday lives crowd him out.

It's all too easy to put off thinking about Jesus. Somehow it doesn't seem as important or pressing as our work or household chores. It doesn't seem to matter if we put God off until we've got more time. But that time soon passes. Children become teenagers, start work or college, and before long they're adults. Then they get married, have children of their own who grow up . . . suddenly retirement and old age start to loom over the horizon, and a lifetime has gone by. The very fact that Christmas is so hectic should warn us that we need to spend time thinking about God as well as all the other preparations, otherwise they'll distract us from it's real message. God wants to speak to us now, to love him now and accept the forgiveness he offers us through Jesus' death and resurrection.

When we get out of bed we take off our night clothes and put on something suitable for the day's activities. Everyone would think we'd lost our senses if we turned up at school or the office in pyjamas! Similarly Paul says that we should 'clothe ourselves with the Lord Jesus Christ' – the way we live and behave is like a uniform which identifies us as belonging to Jesus. We want other people to wake up to Jesus too, by seeing the difference he's made to our lives. If we're awake spiritually and spend time with him each day, they won't be able to avoid noticing!

Prayer
Lord Jesus, we are sorry
for the times when we shut our eyes to you
and don't wake up
to what you are doing with our lives.
Please give us strength
to live every day in your light,
and help other people to see you
and come to love you too.
Amen.

For Younger Children: Talk about the different things we have to do when we get out of bed and make ourselves ready for the new day. Emphasise doing them at the right time, to avoid a rush and the mistakes which result.

To Discuss: What sort of 'clothes' would Jesus like to see in our behaviour? Would other people notice?

Tuesday: Open Your Eyes!

Reading: John 9:1-11

Have you ever thought how much work your eyes have to do? Even a 'simple' activity like reading, writing, or watching TV demands a great deal of them – when it comes to shopping in a supermarket or driving a car they take in a vast amount of information in a very short time. No wonder they get tired and ache sometimes! But unless we have particular problems with our eyesight we take it mostly for granted, even though we'd fear losing it more than any other sense. Without eyesight people are dependent and vulnerable, even today, when so much is done for the handicapped to enable them to live a normal life.

In Jesus' day a handicap like blindness had far more serious consequences than it does now. It's bad enough not being able to see, but 2,000 years ago you'd have been written off as a sinner who deserved punishment. The best you could hope for would be to eke out a living begging for money or food. That's how the blind man in today's reading existed. He wasn't very old, but already he'd realised that he could have no expectation of leading a normal life, or even of having friends and enjoying himself.

In one go Jesus dealt with all that. He smeared some mud on the man's eyes (which was thought by people in those days to be a medicine) and told him to wash it off in the pool at Siloam. The change was dramatic – so much so that when the man went home, some of the neighbours refused to believe it was really him! Jesus did more than restore his eyesight. He gave him a whole new life of earning his living and doing what other people could do, and he made them realise that God was at work in him. The religious leaders were angry, but in their way they were as blind as the man had been. They chose not to look at what God was doing through his Son, so they missed out on all that Jesus could have offered them.

Jesus wants us to know that he's the 'Light of the World' who can help us to see spiritually. When he shines on our lives he shows us all the things that need to be put right – and he deals with them, if we let him. Because of his death, we can receive

16

healing, forgiveness and a completely new start. We don't have to stumble around in the darkness, however. Like the blind man, we can't sort out our own problems, but Jesus offers us new sight and a new life. That's why Christmas is a time of really good news!

Prayer
Lord Jesus,
you gave the blind man sight
and made his life whole again.
We ask you to open our eyes
to see you as you really are,
and change our lives around completely,
so that we can share the good news
of your healing power with everyone we meet.
Amen.

For Younger Children: Play an observation game, such as 'I-Spy', or count how many things you can see, beginning with the letter S, without moving your head or eyes. Explain the complexity of eyesight, and how eyes send messages to the brain. If possible, talk about 'seeing' (or understanding) with our minds.

To Discuss: What has Jesus 'opening your eyes' helped you to understand?

Wednesday: Look Where You're Going!

Reading: Isaiah 2:1-5

The other day I lost my pen. I hunted all over the house for it, without any success. Eventually I asked my wife if she'd seen it anywhere. 'It's here in the kitchen' she replied, 'I wish you'd use your eyes sometimes!'. There isn't much wrong with my eyesight, but I don't always use it properly, especially when I've lost something. We often fail to see all we might because we're not looking carefully enough, or in the right place. It's easy to miss something on TV because we're looking at a magazine or newspaper; and we've all overlooked something we should have done, like paying a bill, because our eyes have been distracted. At this time of year more than any other our eyes are attracted to all kinds of different things – shop displays, bright lights, special TV programmes. It can be hard knowing where to look next! Our inner sight can easily get put off, too, by all the pressures that bear in on our lives. We soon end up not sure where we're supposed to be going or what to do next. Christmas will be a real disappointment if we think about nothing except presents and parties, however much we enjoy them, we feel flat and let down afterwards.

The prophet Isaiah foresaw that one day there would be a whole new world, in which everyone would acknowledge God as the one true God and worship him alone; in it there would be no more warfare or conflict. But his readers certainly never experienced it. The trouble was, they weren't walking in the light of the Lord, so they couldn't see where they were going. They were always stumbling and tripping up, because they refused to obey God and let him direct their ways. Through his prophets God gave them chance after chance to follow him, but they always returned to doing what they wanted to.

Before long the Christmas cards start to arrive (perhaps one or two have already) and many of them will have a picture of a baby in a manger, watched by his parents and a few farm animals. We have to see beyond that, however, to the Cross where the same person died thirty three years later.

18

All of us have the potential to see what God wants to do in our lives, but if we don't look properly, all we'll see is a baby. God wants us to see Jesus as his Son, who lived as a human being, died as a criminal and was raised from death to be King of all.

Prayer
Lord Jesus,
we're sometimes very short-sighted
and miss the things you want to show us
because we're too busy
with our immediate concerns.
Please help us not to be so easily distracted,
but to concentrate on where
you are leading us.
Amen.

For Younger Children: Talk about the results of not looking where we're going. Maybe a recent accident will bring the point home!

To Discuss: What sorts of thing have distracted us from Jesus this week?

Thursday: Do As You're Told!

Reading: Luke 12:35-48

When I was a boy it was always the same – if I had to go and tidy my room or get on with my piano practice I invariably had it in mind to do something else. But however hard I tried to get my own way, I was sent off to do as I'd been told. It was a real nuisance, (or so it seemed at the time). Now I'm a bit older I realise how important it was that my parents made me concentrate on my homework and piano practice. Most of us find it rather difficult always to do what we're told. We like to think we know best and can do it on our own. But when things don't go as they should, as often as not it's because we haven't listened to what we were told, or obeyed instructions.

It isn't just children who have to do as they're told. Anyone who works for someone else has to obey the company rules and do what is expected of him, or her. Employees who don't do what they're paid to do soon lose their jobs. Jesus' parable in today's reading is about servants who've been told what to do by their employer. He's gone off for a while, but they've no idea when he'll get back. So they have to be sure to do their duties properly in case he returns and finds them doing something else – or nothing at all! The fact that the boss isn't watching them all the time doesn't mean they can get away with whatever they want to do. He's not going to be at all pleased if they abuse the responsibility they've been given as soon as his back's turned.

We're servants, because God's given us responsibilities too. If we say we belong to his Kingdom then we must act as though we're ready for Jesus to return at any time. Advent isn't just a time for remembering Jesus' first coming as a baby, but for reminding ourselves as well that one day he'll come back as our King. When that happens it'll be pretty obvious who's really following him, and who isn't. Good servants will do as they've been told, and fulfil their responsibilities for their master. If we're serving Jesus and doing what he wants of us, we can look forward to his coming again, because we'll be properly ready.

It doesn't matter whether we're important and famous or completely unknown. We may be clever with our minds or our hands, brilliant at Maths or hopeless at Art. We'll all be tested against the same standards. And they're tough! None of us comes up to God's requirements, because we prefer to do our own thing and go our own way. But if we put our lives in God's hands he's promised us his Holy Spirit to help us and give us strength to live his way day by day. That way it's no hardship to obey him – in fact we find it's the way to be free, and to be the sort of people that deep down we'd most like to be.

> **Prayer**
> Heavenly Father,
> we're sorry that we don't always do as we're
> told, but try to go our own way.
> We need your Holy Spirit
> to help us do
> the things which please you,
> and keep us ready for when you come again.
> We ask you to send him to us now.
> **Amen.**

For Younger Children: There's a good chance that a recent incident will enable you to explain about the importance of obedience. Talk about warning signs (e.g. on roads). Make your own signs and put them near things which are dangerous (e.g. *Danger – HOT* by a fire). Explain the importance of obeying warnings and doing as we're told.

To Discuss: Why do we find obeying God difficult?

Friday: Behave Yourselves!

Reading: 1 Thessalonians 3:12-4:2

There are two things that Mums and Dads say more than anything else. One is 'Do as you're told', which we thought about yesterday, and the other is 'Behave yourself!'. I used to be told to behave myself when I was acting stupidly, or making other people cross. I hated it at the time, but now I know that I had to learn to act in ways which considered other people as well as me. Throwing a ball around is great in the park, but parents aren't usually too keen on it in the sitting room; the playground's a nice place for shouting and letting off steam, but teachers aren't best pleased if children do it in the classroom! No children like having to learn how to be polite, talk to people pleasantly, hold a knife and fork the right way and all the other things that grown-ups find so important – but if they refuse to learn them, they'll have few friends and find life rather miserable. It's a shame that being told to behave ourselves sounds so negative, but that's only because we're usually doing something we shouldn't when we're told. Actually it's very positive, because that's how we learn to develop good relationships.

When Paul wrote to the Christians at Thessalonica he said 'Behave yourselves!' in a very positive way. It wasn't that the Christians there were badly behaved at table, or rude to each other – in fact Paul praises their good behaviour – but they still needed to carry on behaving in the right way, to show they loved God and wanted to please him. That wouldn't have been easy for the Thessalonians. They lived in Greece, which at that time was a largely pagan country. Even though they were only a small group, their actions were noticed and made an impression on the people around them who'd never heard of Jesus. The same's true today. We too just have to be willing to be a bit different, even at Christmas.

We don't have to do without presents – but we could spend a little less on them so that we can give more to those who have none. We can enjoy our parties but we can enjoy worshipping God in church with his family too. We can share with our families, our friends and neighbours, what Christmas really means to us, so that they can come to know Jesus for themselves. When God tells us to behave ourselves, it's not to obey a set of rules, but to live in a way which tells everyone how much he loves us, and how much we want them to experience his love.

Prayer
Lord Jesus,
you loved us enough to die
so that we could be forgiven
for all the wrong we do.
Please fill us with your love
so that we want to behave
in ways that
show our love for you.
Amen.

For Younger Children: Discuss behaving in the right way at the right time – that what's acceptable in one situation is bad somewhere else. Emphasise that good behaviour is a way of showing we love someone, not just a set of rules.

To Discuss: What sort of behaviour might show people that we're part of God's Kingdom?

23

Saturday: Don't Give Up!

Reading: Revelation 2:8-11

What's your least favourite activity? The way you answer that question depends on who you are and what you have to do. When I was at school I never really got on with swimming or rugby – as often as I could I tried to get out of them! Other children love any sort of sport, but loathe French or Physics. Some Dads detest gardening, while others can't bear the thought of repairing the car. Not every Mum's a keen cook, and many more would be happy to avoid cleaning the house or watching football on television! The things we dislike most are usually the things we find hard to do or understand – and given half a chance we'd give them up now! It's much easier to do the things we like and feel happy with.

Revelation seems at first sight a funny sort of book, full of rather strange word-pictures and difficult to make sense of. It was written in a code-language, as a letter to Christians who were suffering terrible persecution for their faith. By the end of the first century it had become very hard in many places to live publicly as a Christian – those who did were often killed or ill-treated by the authorities, simply because they followed the way of Jesus. Those who didn't suffer like that would often have to endure economic hardship or ridicule from other folk instead. It would have been very tempting for them to give it all up.

Smyrna (a small church in an area of modern-day Turkey) was both poor and persecuted – the Jewish community told lies about the Christians there, and some of them had already been thrown into prison. John, the writer of this extraordinary letter, wanted to say to them 'Don't give up – keep going!' Since then many Christians have faced death rather than give up their faith in the twentieth century more than ever before. It can be very hard to keep going when we're being threatened or laughed at for following Jesus, and we may feel it's barely worth carrying on. Don't forget that Jesus was tempted to give up when he was praying in the Garden just before his arrest – but he didn't give in. Much as he'd have preferred to avoid the pain of being nailed to a Cross he knew he had to obey his heavenly Father and go through with it. As a result of his death and resurrection he won for us the 'crown of life', so that whatever happens to us here can never affect the life we'll enjoy with him forever in heaven when we die. He's completely taken away the power of sin and death over us and set us free to follow him in his strength. We may never lose our lives because we love and serve Jesus, but knowing that nothing can ever take us away from his love will enable us to carry on living as he wants, whatever other people may think of us or do to us.

Prayer
Lord Jesus, thank you for going
to the Cross to die for us and give us new life.
Thank you for all those who have followed
in your footsteps and been willing
to endure suffering and death for your sake.
Please strengthen our faith,
so that we too will keep going for you,
even when we feel like giving up.
Amen.

For Younger Children: What are the things they find most difficult? Talk about perseverance and the need to keep going when things get hard. Think of something impossibly difficult to do (such as a hundred press-ups in a minute!) Talk about why they found it difficult, and explain that even grown-ups find some things difficult. Stress the need to keep going when things are hard.

To Discuss: Try to think of some Christian martyrs and talk about what it was in their situation that led to their willingness to suffer and die for Jesus' sake.

Second Sunday in Advent: A Focus

Reading: Mark 1:9-15

It seems ages since the summer holidays, doesn't it? Can you remember anything about what you did this summer? If you've forgotten, it's a great idea to get out a photograph album with the pictures of past summer holidays and remind yourself of what a good time you had, or how ghastly it was in the rain! The older the photos are, the more interesting and amusing they become –we all laugh when we see what we looked like twenty years ago! Many people are happy to take their holiday snaps on a very simple camera that does everything for them, but some prefer to use one with a focus they can adjust themselves. They keep turning the focusing ring round until the picture they see through the viewfinder is clear and sharp. If they don't, they'll end up with fuzzy, indistinct pictures, and everyone will ask, 'What's that? Grandma's hat?' or, 'Is that an ice-cream Billy's eating?' or even, 'Oh dear, Jane's lost her head!' It's not much use as a photo if no-one knows what it's meant to be!

Mark wrote his gospel so that his readers would have a very clear picture of Jesus. Not of what he looked like, but of what he said and did. Jesus had gone back to heaven to be with his Father, and his disciples were getting older, so Mark may have asked Peter to tell him everything he could remember about Jesus. He would have checked his facts, too, so that no-one could say he was being inaccurate. But above all he wanted us not just to know the truth about Jesus, but why it's so important for us. Like Matthew, Luke, and John, Mark wants us to understand Jesus' relationship with God; why he came to earth to share our life; why he had to die for us; and how that can make a difference to the way we live. He doesn't give us details of Jesus' birth, but he leaves us in no doubt that the baby of Bethlehem grew up to be the most important person this world has ever seen – God's own Son. Sadly, lots of misunderstandings have occurred because people haven't got a clear picture of who Jesus is, or what he said and did. Instead, they try to make up their own picture of him.

The gospels were written so that we can see him properly, and recognise why he matters so much to us.

When we get a clear view of Jesus, we start to understand something of what our Father God's like, too. Jesus couldn't have said and done what he did unless he was God's Son. Once we've got Jesus into focus, the Christian faith starts to make a lot more sense – and makes all the difference to the way we live day by day.

Prayer
Lord Jesus, please help us to see clearly
who you really are;
not just a baby in a manger,
but God's own Son,
who lived with us, died for us,
and now reigns
in heaven as our risen Lord.
Amen.

For Younger Children: Using an old photograph album, talk about recognising people. Discuss which shots are well or poorly taken (e.g. out-of-focus, or Grandad's teeth missing!) Children are fascinated about what Jesus looked like, so clarify that the gospels tell us what sort of person he was, not about his appearance.

To Discuss: Talk about what Jesus might have been like if you'd known him. Check whether the Bible agrees with your view.

Monday: Starting Point

Reading: Jeremiah 1:1-8

Well, it's the start of a new week, so you probably can't wait to get going and see what it brings – or maybe you'd rather wait! There's something about a Monday morning that seems to keep our energy and enthusiasm in first gear, if not in neutral! Some weeks are really exciting, of course, and we wake up on Monday morning raring to go, but there aren't so many of those. On the whole, starting a new week is something we don't find easy. In fact, starting anything new is a challenge. However much we look forward to a new school or job, or moving to a new house, we're also a bit apprehensive. We can't be quite certain how it'll work out, or whether the new situation will live up to our expectations. If we have a choice in the matter, we think carefully before moving house or changing jobs.

Everything in life has to start somewhere – a relationship, a race, even life itself. Jeremiah was pretty clear about where his ministry as a prophet had begun. He knew for sure that even before he was born God had called him, and set him apart to be a prophet, giving God's message to other people. But it didn't come naturally to him. He was a rather quiet man, with no taste for doing things in the public eye. His personality seemed totally at odds with his calling. Because he was shy and unassuming he tried to make excuses to God about how unsuitable he was. It made no difference. God reassured him that he really had called him to this work, and promised him all the strength and courage he'd need to go through with it. The prophetic ministry was no easy task. One of the reasons we sometimes find it hard to change, or start something new, is that we prefer the familiarity and comfort of what we're doing now. But when God calls us to serve him in any capacity (no, he doesn't only call clergy and missionaries!) We can never escape his hand pointing us in the right direction, and holding us tight when the going gets tough. Starting out is often the most difficult part. We worry about what might happen if it goes wrong or doesn't turn out as it should, about what other people will say, about whether we'll be good enough. But as we set out with God on what he's given us to do, we discover very soon that we needn't have worried, that he's with us all the time, guiding us onward.

Advent is the start of the Church's year, and it's a very good time to reflect on where God may be leading us. Perhaps it'll be a starting point for us, a time to move forward in a new direction. It may disrupt our lives, and like Jeremiah we'll be tempted to make all kinds of excuses. That's the time to trust God and take the plunge, knowing his Holy Spirit is always with us – like the coming week, it will turn out far better than we'd feared!

Prayer
Lord Jesus,
we want to serve you
but get worried
about the consequences.
We need your help to overcome
our fears and follow you.
Give us courage to do your will,
and peace in our hearts,
because you're in control.
Amen.

For Younger Children: If there's a recent experience of a new school or playgroup talk about the uncertainty of what it would be like. The same principle would apply to any anticipated new activity or experience. Explain that once we've started something it's rarely as bad as we feared.

To Discuss: What have you found difficult to start and why? What new direction might God be leading you in now?

Tuesday: Help On The Way

Reading: John 16:12-16

'It's the only way to learn – so jump in at the deep end'! What a way to start swimming! It's a terrifying thought, but the best way to learn anything is actually to do it. You can find out any amount about the techniques of swimming, why your body floats, or who won the 200 metre backstroke gold medal at the last Olympics, but until you're in the water you won't discover how to swim yourself. The same is true of many other things – you learn to drive when you get behind the steering wheel, you learn to play the clarinet by starting to blow into one, and you pick up how to speak in public by standing up and speaking. It can feel a bit lonely, especially if what you've got to do can't be done by anyone else, but it's much better if you know someone else is there to support and help you. Even so, we'd all rather put off having to do something like that for as long as possible, given half the chance! But once we've had a go and discovered we can do it, we wonder why we were so worried!

Yesterday we saw how Jeremiah must have felt when God told him to give his message to the people of Israel. Jesus, too, would have had some very human qualms as he set out on the three years of ministry he knew would lead to his death. We don't need to feel guilty if we're a bit anxious over what God's called us to do.

In today's reading, Jesus is explaining to his disciples that however much they fear his coming death and resurrection, and return to his Father in Heaven, he won't leave them to 'sink or swim'. It may feel as though they're being thrown in at the deep end, but God will be there with them by his Holy Spirit. The Holy Spirit is God's presence with us all the time, giving us the strength and will to serve him, however anxious we may feel. In this century, many Christians and churches have rediscovered the power of the Holy Spirit in their lives and experience. Without him we can achieve nothing – we need him every day to fill our lives with Jesus' love and to help us as we serve him. It's the Holy Spirit who enables us to understand what God wants of us, he

30

gives us the strength to persevere. That's how we continue the work of God's Kingdom, until Jesus returns in glory.

> **Prayer**
> Lord God,
> we know we can't do anything
> on our own without your help.
> We ask your Holy Spirit
> to live within us
> so that we can recognise
> what you call us to do,
> and be able to see it through.
> **Amen.**

For Younger Children: Have a competition, where parents learn how to do forward rolls or improve their handwriting, while children learn something adult (like how to use a typewriter). Explain that however hard we may find something, God will always help us.

To Discuss: What difference does the Holy Spirit make to our lives day by day?

Wednesday: Promises, Promises!

Reading: 2 Peter 3:8-14

Whenever I go into a sweet-shop to buy a bar of chocolate it takes me ages to make up my mind which one I want. Perhaps you've got a favourite, but I can never decide whether I prefer a a Coconut Cream, a Toffee Crisp or a Turkish Delight! Some years ago Turkish Delight bars were advertised with the slogan, 'Full of eastern promise'. I'm still not quite sure what eastern promise is, or why it's different to western promise, but the advert certainly gave the promise that if you chose the Turkish Delight, you would be in for a gastronomic thrill as soon as you tasted it! A promise always looks forward to the future, to something which hasn't yet happened, but we can anticipate with pleasure. That's true of a bar of chocolate, of a planned visit or a forthcoming event. We believe that what's been promised will come about because someone's given their word to it. If the promise isn't fulfilled we feel let down. If the chocolate we've bought isn't as good as its wrapper claims, we haven't had good value for money. If someone says they'll do something for us but never gets round to it, we wonder whether they really care. Of course, we forget to keep the promises we make sometimes, and then other people feel we've let them down.

During Advent we remember some of the promises God's made to us. There are quite a lot of them, but one is that Jesus will return to this earth and create a completely different heaven and earth, where there'll be no more sadness or bitterness, violence or hatred. In this new heaven and earth everything will be at peace. The second letter of Peter was written to encourage Christians who were being persecuted and in great danger. Perhaps some of them thought God wasn't keeping his promises or didn't mean what he said. But Peter wanted to remind them that just as God had kept his promise to send his Son to our world as a baby, so he'll also keep his word about Jesus returning in glory.

God has kept every single promise he made, so we can be sure that he really will come back to the world as King of all.

When he does, he'll bring all who love him to his Kingdom, the new heaven and earth, where nothing bad can exist. Because of Jesus' first coming we can look forward to his second coming with joy. The first Christians couldn't wait for Jesus to return, and looked for any sign that it was about to happen. We can too, because we know that God always keeps his word.

Prayer
Thank you, Heavenly Father,
for always keeping
your promises.
We're sorry that so often we fail
to do what we've said we will.
Please help us to trust you
to fulfil your word
and look forward
to your greatest promise that
one day we'll live with you
for ever.
Amen.

For Younger Children: Talk about promises and how we often fail to keep them. Make a promise that you'll keep right through the day (adults too). Explain how God always keeps his promises.

To Discuss: Which promise from God are you looking forward to most of all?

Thursday: Right Turn

Reading: Isaiah 55:6-11

Have you ever got lost because you took the wrong turning? It can ruin a day out or holiday, especially if you take a couple of hours to get back to where you should have been! Paddington Bear once got the Brown family hopelessly lost by telling them to turn left at a piece of marmalade peel, which made the whole family very irritable! When we get lost while driving, the conversation goes a bit like this: 'Are you sure this is the right way to go?' 'Yes, of course it is. We turned left just by the Donkey and Carrot.' 'Well it doesn't look right to me.' 'Ah, hang on. I think we should have gone straight over at that big roundabout'. 'There's a road sign just ahead saying Stockport'. 'Turn left there and cut across ....' Five minutes later we're hopelessly lost! The important thing to do if you know you've taken a wrong turning is to go back to where you went wrong. That way you know you've put the mistake right. If you try to find some other way there's a pretty good chance you'll end up even more lost.

When Isaiah wrote the words in today's reading the Israelites had been in exile in Babylon for many years. Only the older generation could remember what it had been like in the Promised Land. Over the years they'd got more and more 'lost' in their refusal to obey God's laws. Instead of worshipping him they were worshipping all sorts of other strange idols and doing terrible things that God had completely forbidden. Every now and then they'd try to put things right but only got themselves into a worse mess. They were so stubborn that they wouldn't return to God, and the result was that they spent seventy years away from their country in Babylon, a land ruled by a heathen king called Nebuchadnezzar. There seemed to be no hope.

Isaiah knew that God wanted to give his people the chance to turn back to him and set off again in the right direction. If only they'd seek him and realise how much he longed to forgive them! Despite all they'd done wrong he still wanted to give them another opportunity to get back on the right track. As we come through Advent towards Christmas we can recognise the opportunity that God gives us to make the right turn. We can be sure that the way he leads us in is the best. If we try to find our own way we're guaranteed to get into a worse muddle, and further from where God wants us to be. If we turn to him and admit that we've gone wrong, he's only too willing to show us the right path – and walk along it with us too!

Prayer
Lord God,
please help us to see
when we've gone our own way
and got ourselves 'lost'
from where you want us to be.
We ask you to guide us
in the right paths
and keep us true to your ways.
Amen.

For Younger Children: Find a road map, and if they're old enough play a game of finding the best way to a destination. Explain how important it is to go the right way and what to do when we get lost. Show how God keeps us going in the right direction if we follow his ways.

To Discuss: Why is it so hard to admit that we've made a mistake or gone the wrong way? How can we be certain what is the right way to go?

Friday: Hope For Better Things

Reading: Isaiah 40:1-5

It's no fun being hopeless! When someone says you are, you get the idea you might as well give up now. What they mean is that they can't see any prospect of you ever getting any better. I was hopeless at Physics at school – I never could understand it and I was only too glad to finish with it. I'm hopeless at mending cars, too: no-one in their right mind would ever let me loose on a car engine! Perhaps you're hopeless at French, or sport, or playing the euphonium; but you certainly aren't hopeless at everything. It's one thing to have the odd weak spot but if there really isn't any hope at all for you, tomorrow's is hardly worth waiting for!

Today's reading in the prophet Isaiah comes, like yesterday's, from the time when God's people were in exile. After so many years of having to obey the kings of Babylon, they were despairing of ever being able to see again the Promised Land, the country God had given them. It must have felt like the end of the world to be taken away from it. In fact, after fifty years or more, very few of the people would have been old enough to remember what Jerusalem was like. The younger ones probably felt more at home in Babylon. But they weren't free, and it wasn't the place God had given them. Deep down they knew they belonged in Israel. So God gave them a message through his prophet that things weren't hopeless – things would get better. They'd be going back home!

The world we live in now can seem a sad place, full of problems and unhappiness. Many people despair of finding any meaning or lasting happiness in it. But God has promised that one day he'll do something about it, so that everyone will recognise his glory and worship him. God never forgets or breaks his promises. He promised the Israelites that however bad yesterday had been, there was the opportunity today to allow God to lead them into a better tomorrow. In Jesus he makes the same promise to us. We don't need to feel our way in the darkness or look back at the past all the time, because we can look confidently to the future knowing that we're in God's hands.

Advent is an ideal time for remembering all that God's

promised us, and how in Jesus we can see those promises fulfilled. We know that Jesus is the Light of the World, and we can be more than just hopeful that there'll be better things to come. So much better that we can't imagine how wonderful they'll be!

> **Prayer**
> Heavenly Father,
> we sometimes get worried
> and upset about the things
> that happen in our world.
> Thank you for
> promising us a place
> in your Kingdom
> for ever.
> Please help us not to forget
> that one day you're going
> to put right
> all that's bad and evil.
> **Amen**

For Younger Children: There should be some experience of illness which you can draw on to talk about 'getting better'. Alternatively you could discuss how practice helps us to 'get better' at a particular activity. Ask them what things in the world could be made better and explain that one day God will make everything better.

To Discuss: Some people say that looking forward to a better future with God is just escapism. How would you answer them?

Saturday: Finishing The Job

Reading: Philippians 1:1-11

Do you find it's easier to start a job or finish it? On a hot summer's day I can get quite enthusiastic about finding the lawn-mower and doing something to make the garden look tidier. Unfortunately, after half an hour's work someone calls me in to have a cold drink, and going back out to finish the job becomes a lot harder! Perhaps you find, like me, that you're just in the middle of something when the doorbell or telephone rings. By the end of the conversation I've totally forgotten what I was supposed to be doing, only to realise two days later that I never finished off the job!

There are all sorts of reasons why we start off certain jobs but don't get them finished. Perhaps it's taking longer than we thought, or it's more difficult than we'd anticipated, maybe we've been distracted by something more interesting or less demanding. Paul wanted the Christians in the church at Philippi to learn that they had to 'finish the job'. Along with many of the early churches they suffered persecution and ridicule: Paul himself was in prison when he wrote this letter. The temptation to give up on the Christian faith they'd started must have been very strong. There were plenty of alternatives that seemed a lot less demanding.

Being a Christian, a follower of Jesus, isn't an easy option. Paul knew that from his own experience, and so he prayed every day that the Philippian Christians would grow in their understanding and love of Jesus. That way they would be strengthened and enabled to face whatever happened, and to witness to Jesus until his return. We're still waiting for him, and looking forward to the time when his kingdom will finally and completely be brought in. Until then we may have to put up with people thinking we're a bit quaint, laughing at us or even treating us badly. That's exactly what they did to Jesus. However, he had a job to complete – and when he said 'It's finished' as he hung on the Cross, he meant that he'd done all that God had sent him to do. He went through with his work to the bitter end. He did it because he loved us that much, and knew there was no other way

38

for us to become part of God's Kingdom. As we respond to his love we can find strength to follow his example and finish whatever God gives us to do.

> **Prayer**
> Lord Jesus,
> you finished the work
> your Father gave you to do
> by dying for us.
> Give us the strength
> and commitment
> to carry on following you,
> and not be put off by
> any opposition or difficulties.
> **Amen.**

For Younger Children: Finishing something off isn't easy for most children, so pick out the sort of activity that needs to be finished properly, such as a job in the household like washing up, and let them work out what happens if it isn't completed. Describe how God wants us to finish what he's given us to do for him. Look back to Tuesday's competition, and see if anyone's improved their performance. Explain the importance of finishing what we're given to do, and how Jesus did everything his Father had told him to.

To Discuss: What sort of Christian service often gets left half-done? Why do you think that sometimes happens?

Third Sunday in Advent: A Message

Reading: Luke 1:5-17

Has there been a big change in your life recently? We had to move house a little while ago, which meant a new place to live, a new job, a new school, new friends and learning to live in the country after living in towns. It's been great fun, but we wouldn't want to do it too often! Big changes like that don't happen very often. Most changes are small and easier to deal with. Others only happen once or twice in a lifetime, such as getting married or having a baby arrive in the household. Of all the changes in life that must be the biggest, especially if it's the first baby. There are new routines to get into, disturbed nights, babysitting, different feeding times. The list is endless!

The arrival of a child wasn't quite what Zechariah and Elizabeth were expecting. They were beyond the age when that sort of thing happened. Elizabeth was sad, because in those days people regarded it as a disgrace not to be able to have children, but she was probably used to that. Zechariah was a priest who was taking his turn to serve in the Temple at Jerusalem. He'd been chosen to go right inside the Temple to burn incense in the worship of God. It was a special honour to do this and no priest could do it more than once in his lifetime. So this really was the high point of Zechariah's career. The last thing he, or anyone else, was expecting was a dramatic change in his life.

Things didn't work out exactly as planned. As Zechariah went about this special duty, God started to speak to him. That was a big enough shock, but nothing when compared to the message! The angel who appeared by the altar told him that he was going to be a Dad (which he'd long since given up as wishful thinking) and his son would have a unique part to play in God's plan.

Like Zechariah, we like to feel comfortable and safe, to be in control of events, and not disturbed or disrupted from what we want to do. We soon become complacent and forget that God is in control, so when he speaks to us it can come as a bit of a surprise. It catches us unawares, because we aren't expecting him to turn our lives upside down. But following Jesus means letting him do things his way, and being open to hearing his voice whenever he calls us. Sometimes the Christian life involves doing something for reasons we can't understand, or having all our careful plans upset. Only when we look back can we see that God's ways were infinitely better than ours. At the time Zechariah had no idea how God would use him and Elizabeth to be a key part of his plan to save us from the consequences of our sinfulness and selfishness. He had to act in faith. That's what God calls all his people to do.

> **Prayer**
> Lord God,
> please help us to listen
> to what you say to us,
> and give us the faith
> to do whatever you ask of us,
> even when we find it hard
> to understand.
> **Amen.**

For Younger Children: Ask what has given them a shock and how they felt afterwards. Emphasise the surprise element rather than fright, and try to enable them to understand how Zechariah felt when he encountered the angel. Explain how God sometimes comes to us unexpectedly with a message.

To Discuss: How can we know when God's speaking to us? What might prevent us from hearing him clearly?

Monday: Lost For Words

Reading: Luke 1:18-25

It's very awkward to break news to someone if you know they won't believe you. You work out in your mind just how to make the message convincing, but when you actually tell them, it doesn't work at first. You may need to try several ways of explaining before the penny drops! Zechariah must have been wondering how to get it across to Elizabeth that she was going to have a baby boy. He wasn't entirely sure about it himself! After all, his wife was too old now to have children, and anyway, what proof did he have that God wasn't just testing him? Perhaps it was all imagination. Gabriel left him in no doubt about this wonderful news, but Zechariah wouldn't really believe him. It wasn't that Zechariah's doubts made any difference to God's plans, but to show him that God really meant what he said, Gabriel told him he wouldn't be able to speak till the baby had arrived.

All this time the crowds were outside, wondering what on earth was going on in the Temple. Zechariah had been in there for ages; far longer than normal. When he emerged, it was very clear he'd had a close encounter of the divine kind. God had affected him powerfully and he could only communicate in sign language. Once his duties were over he was probably very glad to go home and be quiet for a while (not that he had much choice!) It wasn't long before Elizabeth found she was expecting a baby – and like any Mum-to-be she was delighted. More so, because for her this was a sign that God had shown her his favour, despite her age.

It's easy to get carried away with our own ideas about what God should do and how he ought to do it. God has his own ways which are far better than ours, and even if they don't make sense straight away, we realise later that they're an essential part of his plans. Zechariah thought he'd go down in history as a priest; Elisabeth thought she'd be forgotten in disgrace. Instead, God made them the parents of John the Baptist, the prophet who prepared the way for Jesus. We remember John in Advent because he was the one who announced the coming of King Jesus. We also remind ourselves of his Mum and Dad, who in spite of their age and their doubts obeyed God and acted in faith, to become part of his plan to bring salvation to the world. Even when God takes us by surprise and leaves us lost for words, all that's needed for his plans to come to fulfilment is our obedience.

Prayer
Father God,
thank you that you want to use
people like us
to be a part of your plan
for the world.
Help us,
like Zechariah and Elizabeth,
to obey you in faith
and leave the results to you.
Amen.

For Younger Children: Plan a family event together (how about the Christmas shopping?) and if possible do it! If not, plan a hypothetical holiday or trip. Talk about God's plan for each of our lives which he wants us to follow.

To Discuss: What sort of preconceived ideas do we have that make us doubt what God says to us?

Tuesday: Another Message

Reading: Luke 1:26-38

The Christmas cards are coming thick and fast now. The postmen are in the middle of the busiest time in their year, and everyone's writing to friends and relatives, often for the first time since last Christmas! What sort of messages do people send you? The ones printed in the cards are all right, but they're not very personal, and it feels much more friendly if someone's put a letter inside. You find out what's been happening to them and that they're still interested in you. Somehow Christmas is a time for messages of all sorts, whether it's a personal letter, or the Queen's message to the Commonwealth. Usually the words try to convey hope and joy, even if there's been bad news during the year.

Gabriel was doing a lot of work delivering God's messages, rather like the postmen. Having spoken to Zechariah and given him news that would turn his life and Elizabeth's upside down, he turned his attention to Mary. Unlike Zechariah, Mary wasn't important, or at the peak of her career. She was an ordinary girl, engaged to be married to the local carpenter. A quiet person by nature, she was busy minding her own business, probably getting ready for her wedding day. Suddenly Gabriel appeared with God's message for her, and if Zechariah had been perplexed, Mary was utterly dumbfounded! For a start, why would God send an angel to someone like her – was he cross with her perhaps? Far from it. He was so pleased with her that she was the one he'd chosen to bring into this world as a tiny baby the long-awaited Messiah. Mary was certainly frightened when Gabriel appeared, but she must have been equally alarmed by what she heard. She wasn't even married yet, so how could she have a baby? No doubt all sorts of other fears and impossibilities crossed her mind, but God was at work, and what seemed impossible to her was entirely possible to him. God can do anything. The word 'impossible' means nothing to God.

Mary needed a great deal of courage to obey God. She was worried about what Joseph would think, her friends would probably regard her as an immoral woman. And this baby would need looking after – Mary wasn't properly ready yet for marriage, let alone being a mother. But she took God at his word. He'd promised her his Holy Spirit, and she trusted him to fulfil his purposes in her. Funnily enough, her cousin Elizabeth was also pregnant unexpectedly, so she'd have company. It's never easy to obey God if we're worried about how other people might react to what he's told us to do. If God asks us to serve him, we can be sure he'll keep his promise to give us the Holy Spirit, so that we have the strength and courage to see it through.

> **Prayer**
> Thank you, Father God,
> for Mary's obedience and trust.
> We ask for your
> Holy Spirit to make us
> willing to obey you
> and do your will,
> regardless of what anyone else
> may say.
> **Amen.**

For Younger Children: If you've started to receive Christmas cards, read some of the messages out. Are they good news or bad? Think about the messages you'll write on the Christmas cards you'll send to friends and family. Discuss God's message to Mary and her reaction to it.

To Discuss: How much should we use our 'common sense' in serving God? Can that sometimes be the opposite of true faith?

Wednesday: A Song For Everyone

Reading: Luke 1:46-56

By this stage of Advent, carol services and concerts are in full swing. Even people who never go inside a church love to sing well-known carols. It's a joyful time of year and singing is one of the best ways to show we're happy. We don't need music to live, yet no-one can imagine life without it. Somehow it expresses our feelings in a deep way, and adds something inexplicable to ordinary words. People sing at football matches (well, they do if their team's winning!) at political rallies, at parties. If they're Welsh they'll sing anywhere and create the most glorious sound! Christians have also used songs and hymns to praise God for thousands of years, in expressing their feelings about God and his love. Nearly a thousand years before Jesus was born, the Psalms started to be written as a way for all God's people to join together in praiseing him and praying to him. Mary would have known that tradition, and her song in today's reading is based on it.

There's a great deal of singing and praise in the Christmas story. Mary wasn't the only one who sang. The angels sang from the sky, the shepherds sang in the fields, and Zechariah sang as soon as he got his voice back! Mary's song is for everyone. All those who know God hasn't forgotten them or left them on one side, who recognise what great things he's done for them, will want to sing with her. It's a song about God's mercy, his mighty acts, his help, and his favour towards the poor and humble. For Mary it reminded her of how God had dealt with her own nation, the Israelites, but ever since then Christians have realised how the coming of Jesus to our world means the same is true for all.

It's a shame when people only sing Christmas carols, though. Praising God isn't just something to do at Christmas. He wants us to sing our praises to him all the time, whatever we're doing, wherever we are. There's nothing more important we can ever do! God deserves our worship and praise and love anyway, for all he's done for us. When we're thinking about his love and goodness it stops us dwelling on our problems and moaning about them! Why not sing some carols at work or school, or even at home to remind you of all that God did in sending Jesus, his Son, into the world. Perhaps you know some new ones, too, as well as the familiar ones. You could even try to write your own!

> **Prayer**
> Heavenly Father,
> we want to sing your praise
> because you loved us enough
> to send Jesus to be our Saviour.
> Help us not just to sing to you in church,
> but fill our hearts with praise and worship
> whatever we're doing.
> **Amen.**

For Younger Children: Sing a well-known carol together, and see how it praises God in its words and music. Encourage singing to God throughout the day.   You could make a tape of carols for someone who's housebound, as a Christmas gift.

To Discuss: If you were writing a Christmas carol, what part of the story would you want to emphasise most?

Thursday: Whoever Gave That Name?

Reading: Luke 1:57-66+80

There really are some extraordinary names to be found. It's nice to have an unusual name, but some are downright embarrassing. Do you know anyone who has a name they won't tell? If you look in *The Times* 'Birth Announcements' column you'll probably see quite a few names that make you think, 'Whoever gave them a name like that?' Many of them are connected with ancestors and the family, but some are based on a personal whim. They can seem positively outlandish, like the man who named his child after the entire Liverpool football team (what a pity it was a girl)! Names are very important. They give us an identity, and often have a particular meaning: my name means a 'steward' or 'servant'. Occasionally people dislike their names so much that they have them legally changed by deed poll to something more acceptable.

Most parents discuss their baby's names long before it arrives. Unfortunately Zechariah couldn't speak, which must have affected the discussion somewhat! However, choice was more limited in those days, and apart from Elizabeth, everyone assumed that they'd follow tradition and call their boy Zechariah, after his Dad. They were all thrilled when Elizabeth's baby finally arrived and yes, it was a boy! Soon it was time to give him a name, which was announced during the ritual of circumcision. But there was consternation when Elizabeth told them his name – John! 'What on earth do you want to call him that for?' said one. 'There aren't any Johns in your family are there?' asked another. Both Elizabeth and Zechariah were quite firm about the name, however. Unlike some parents they were in complete agreement! Then something equally amazing happened – Zechariah's voice came back as soon as he'd written the name down, and suddenly he burst out with praises to God. No wonder the neighbours started talking!

John was a special child, set apart by God to serve him in a unique way. No doubt everyone wondered how he'd grow up and what he would do that was so special. But they were absolutely sure he was called by God. His name and his birth were signs that

God's hand was on him. When we become Christians we're identified as God's people. We don't change our names or get a new personality, but people know that God's hand is on us, too, and that we've been called to serve him.

> **Prayer**
> We thank you, Heavenly Father,
> that we belong to you,
> and can be known
> as your people.
> As we grow in you
> please help us to live
> as you want us to,
> so that other people can see who
> we belong to.
> **Amen.**

For Younger Children: If you know their meaning, talk about the family's names. Emphasise the difference between a Christian name, which identifies the individual, and the surname, which demonstrates the family we belong to. Talk about the meaning of names. Design a symbol for your names, if you can. Explain how being a Christian means we have Jesus' name and belong to him.

To Discuss: How should our behaviour be different from the other people's?

Friday: Second Fiddle

Reading: John 1:6-8/19-28

It takes a lot of practice and hard work to become a good musician. Even then there are some pieces which can only be played well by the very best musicians no-one but a concert performer would attempt them because they're so difficult. Only a tiny handful of those who learn an instrument ever become household names – the rest remain in the orchestra or teaching music, and never make it as a soloist or conductor. They have to be content to stay in the background. The great conductor Arturo Toscanini learnt the cello as a child and by the age of 20 was good enough to join an opera company which was touring the world. He started off as a very ordinary cellist, but one day in Brazil the proper conductor fell ill and at the last minute a substitute had to be found. Arturo could remember the piece so he took the baton – and there was no more playing second fiddle for him after that. But he still needed to learn to play in the orchestra before he could take charge of it.

None of us like to be second fiddle – we prefer to be the centre of attention, rather than see someone else being noticed and applauded by other people. Learning to step back so that someone else can step forward isn't something that comes very easily. John the Baptist had been used to a lot of attention for a long time. People flocked out to the desert, where he lived, to hear him preach. At the same time, he hadn't been called by God to a self-centred ministry. On the contrary, his role was to draw attention to Jesus. Jesus was 30 before he set out on his three years of ministry so until then John had the field to himself. But thereafter he had to stand back for Jesus, because he had finished the great task God had called him to do.

Like John, we've been called to tell others about Jesus, and help them find him. There's no place in the Christian life for self-centredness or attention-seeking. We all have a different part to play in building up God's Kingdom, but our faith is for sharing with our friends and people we meet. It may feel as though others have got more important work than we have, that what we do never gets noticed, but God takes notice of those who obey him. Whatever our specific tasks, all of us have to work together and play second fiddle to Jesus so that people are drawn to him.

> **Prayer**
> Father God, forgive us
> for being more concerned
> with what people think of us
> than with how they respond to you.
> Please help us learn
> how to step back
> so that they are attracted
> to your love and power.
> **Amen.**

For Younger Children: Discuss the ways in which we show off and try to be the centre of attention. Do a role-play of two people being interviewed for a job (or something similar) one very 'pushy', the other very shy. Draw out the ways in which we try to seek attention. Contrast this with John the Baptist's willingness to let Jesus be the focus of attention, and emphasise that what really matters is what God thinks of us.

To Discuss: How can we get in the way of the message of Jesus by the way we think and act?

Saturday: Testimony To John

Reading: Matthew 11:2-11

I've just come back from a presentation ceremony. It was for a schoolteacher who was retiring after many years at the same school. As she was presented with various gifts, those handing them over said various things about how good a teacher she'd been and how much she'd be missed. It was a testimony to her years of hard work as a first-rate teacher. In sport, a great player is often given a 'testimonial' match in which there's a special competition and everyone who takes part recognises the exceptional talents of the star, and is happy for him to get a fair proportion of the takings. It's a testimony to his abilities and to his contribution to the sport over a period of time. A testimony says something quite clear about someone, and how other people regard them.

Unfortunately for John the Baptist, not everyone thought he was great! He certainly had a following, but the religious authorities found him more than a handful, not least because he kept pointing out their faults. To cap it all, he'd condemned King Herod for marrying his brother's wife, and for that he'd been thrown into prison. Herod was a weak character and on his own might not have killed John, but Herodias, the lady in question manipulated and schemed to make sure John was beheaded. Just before his death, John sent a message to Jesus from his prison, asking for proof that he really was the promised Messiah. Jesus replied by simply pointing out the evidence: people were being healed, the blind were given sight, the lame were walking, lepers were cleansed. Then he gave his own testimony to John. Despite the discomforts of his life and imprisonment, John had done exactly what God had wanted him to do. Whatever other people thought, Jesus wanted everyone to know that John had played a central part in God's plan to bring us salvation and forgiveness. Even so, those who follow Jesus will be considered greater than John not because they're any better than him, but because with Jesus' coming a whole new age has dawned.

John was the last of the prophets, the forerunner of Jesus. After him Jesus' arrival would change everything. We too are part of God's new society if we follow Jesus and bear testimony to him.

For Younger Children: Give a testimony for other members of the family, explaining what you think is good about them. Older ones might prefer to do the same for a favourite pop-star or sporting hero. Ask what sort of evidence demonstrates that someone is 'good'. Discuss how we can be a testimony to Jesus.

To Discuss: What's the most important part of the life, death and resurrection of Jesus to tell people about?

Fourth Sunday in Advent: Keep Hoping

Reading: Luke 2:1-7

It's so infuriating when something happens to spoil what we've been looking forward to. Just as we're settling down to our favourite TV programme, the doorbell rings. Much as we like our friends to visit us, we do prefer them not to when it isn't convenient! Maybe you know someone who makes a habit of falling ill the day before they're due to go on holiday. Whenever I'm late for an appointment, there seems to be a traffic jam for me to get stuck in, and if I decide to go by train the signals seem to fail somewhere along the line! There are all sorts of frustrations which upset our careful planning. We often say to ourselves in these sorts of situation, 'Why did it have to happen now?'.

Mary must have felt a bit like that. She wasn't married and she was expecting a baby. She knew that this child would be the one sent by God to bring salvation to the world, but it wasn't too clear to her how this would happen. And like any Mum about to give birth she must have been tired and wishing it would all be over and done with. At least she might have expected to have her baby in the comfort and security of her own home. Unfortunately the Emperor Augustus put paid to that idea, when he had his brainwave – a census. So poor Mary and Joseph had to face a long journey by donkey to Bethlehem on a dusty, bumpy road, just to suit the government! It really was the last straw, but since they had no choice in the matter, off they set. Whether it was the strain of the situation or the uncomfortable journey we don't know, but by the time they were nearing Bethlehem Mary knew the baby was on its way. As soon as they got there, Joseph rushed about, trying to find a room, but with no success. It seemed as if half of Israel had descended on this little town, so in the end they made do with the offer of a stable. Not exactly five-star luxury, but in the circumstances better than nothing. So it was that God's Son was born as a human being to two tired, frustrated and fed up parents who had nowhere to lay him down except an animal's feeding trough. Home was far away, and everyone else had other things on their mind.

But however Mary and Joseph saw it, this was all part of God's plan. Hardly right for the Messiah? Not to our way of thinking, but then God doesn't do things as we would. Mary and Joseph would surely have preferred God to organise things a bit more comfortably. As it was, Jesus' birth took place amid anxiety, discomfort and tiredness. Just because things aren't going well for us, or we feel a bit down in the dumps, we shouldn't assume that God's not doing anything. He often uses the worst times and the bad experiences to teach us and accomplish his will. We may wonder what he's up to, but if we offer him our fear and unhappiness, he will always use them for his glory.

Prayer
Lord Jesus, thank you
for understanding how we feel
when things go wrong
and we're afraid or confused.
Please give us the faith to trust you,
however bad things are,
and show us how you bring
something good from them.
Amen.

For Younger Children: If you have any 'appeal' material (e.g. for Crisis at Christmas or Shelter) talk about people who have a hard time. Very young children might find it easier to relate this to a story such as *Cinderella*. Explain how God is with us in all circumstances, good and bad, and always brings good out of them. If you have a crib, today's an ideal occasion to set it up. You could put figures of Mary and Joseph elsewhere in the room, on a 'journey' to Bethlehem.

To Discuss: Do you know anyone who's having a bad time just now, or is there a situation you know of which seems too awful for anyone to accept? How might God bring about his will in this?

Monday: Songs Of Praise

Reading: Isaiah 12:1-6

Can you imagine life without a TV? Sometimes I think we organise our diary around the programmes we want to see! It's not that long ago that a television set really was a status symbol. When I was small, our family didn't have one, so on a Sunday evening I'd go with my grandmother to the lady next door to watch *Songs of Praise*. Perhaps you watch that programme, because millions of people do! It's changed a bit over thirty years, and now each hymn is chosen by someone who tells us *why* they've chosen it. Often they want to praise God for something he's done in their life, and the hymn reflects that. Praise usually goes back to something that's already been done. Teachers praise their pupils for good work, Parents may praise a tidy bedroom or commend a helpful attitude in the home. It isn't usual to praise someone before they've done something, though!

When Isaiah spoke the words in today's reading, Israel was in a bad way. There was a new superpower just to the north called Assyria, the most powerful nation that had ever been seen in that part of the world. They were strong and ruthless, and everyone was terrified that they'd want to invade Israel and make it their own land. If they did, many people would be killed and those who survived would be treated very harshly. Not much to praise God for, on the face of it. Isaiah had already told the Israelites that being invaded would be the result of their refusal to obey God, and there seemed little doubt that this would happen. But he also wanted to tell them that God wouldn't let the Assyrians get away with cruelty and injustice. One day the Israelites would praise God again, because he was going to save them and restore them to himself. Instead of being angry he'd comfort them. Although they were afraid now, he would bring them security in trusting him. Their fear and despair would turn to joy and praise!

It's exciting to look forward, and Christmas is very close. It's a time for praising God, not just for what he has done (wonderful though that is!) but for all that he's promised to do. We can sing his praises, knowing that he's in control of everything. Jesus' death and resurrection has defeated the forces of sin and evil for ever. When there's bad news around us, we can still praise God. The Israelites would shout aloud and sing because the 'Holy One of Israel' was with them. He's with us, too, all the time. So for all he's done already, all he's doing now, and all he's going to do, *Praise the Lord!*

Prayer
Thank you, Lord God, that you're in
charge of this world,
and that we're in your hands.
Even when things around us make us
sad and anxious
please help us to remember
that you always keep your word.
May we sing and shout your
good news to everyone we meet.
Amen.

For Younger Children: Make up your own family 'Songs of Praise' by having everyone choose their favourite hymn or carol, and explain why they've chosen it. You could sing them at home, but if time allows, why not go carol-singing? You might even raise some donations for your chosen charity!

To Discuss: Which hymn or Christian song sums up for you all you want to praise God for?

Tuesday: First The Good News

Reading: Isaiah 52:7-10

Nearly every morning I wake up at half past six to the sound of the early news. I can't imagine how the presenters get up so early and sound so bright at such an unearthly hour! As often as not the news is political or economic and I turn over for a few minutes' more dozing, but occasionally something that's said wakes me up with a start. Unfortunately it's the bad news that usually does that – like a major disaster or a war. It's not all that often that good news hits the headlines enough to wake me up! Even the good news is sometimes the end result of bad news! We're all glad if a war ends, but we'd have much preferred it not to start!

Israel had had so much bad news they were wondering if there was any good news left! In yesterday's reading we saw how Isaiah had warned them about the Assyrians. They didn't take much notice, and soon afterwards the northern part of Israel was overrun by the terrible enemy. Years later, those who were left in the southern kingdom went into exile in Babylon as a result of their disobedience and stayed there for seventy years. Could there be any news worse than that? How would they know when the news started to get better?

We're used to finding out what's going on in the world by switching on the news bulletins, or picking up a newspaper and reading about it. More than five hundred years before the birth of Jesus, they relied on messengers to keep informed. If an army had fought a battle and won a famous victory, a messenger would be sent back to tell everyone as soon as possible. Without motorways and Inter-City trains he had to ride or run all the way, over mountains and hills, through valleys, across plains, until he'd delivered his priceless message, 'We won!' However tired he felt, however tough the journey, he had to keep going because the news was good. Isaiah saw the message of good news from God in those terms. There was peace and salvation to come, and God was going to bring back his people from exile. Anyone who brought that sort of good news would have been welcomed with open arms!

When he wrote these words near the end of those years in Babylon, Isaiah knew that one day God would intervene decisively in our world, that 'our God reigns', that he's King of all the world, and he would certainly bring peace and salvation. Even the broken-down walls of Jerusalem and the battered shell of the Temple would start to sing, and burst out in songs and shouts of joy. If the news is that good, it's up to us to shout and sing about it so everyone else hears it too!

Prayer
Lord Jesus,
you came to bring us the good news
of forgiveness, salvation and peace
through your victory on the Cross.
We need your strength
to sing and shout about it
to everyone we meet.
Amen.

For Younger Children: Listen to, watch, or read the news, and discuss whether the items are good or bad news. Bear in mind that one person's good news may be bad for someone else! Talk about what's needed to make bad news good. Discuss how the coming of Jesus can bring good news from God into a bad situation by transforming it.

To Discuss: What makes news good rather than bad? What's good about the message of Jesus?

Wednesday: A Safe Place

Reading: Jeremiah 23:3-7

We're all encouraged to be safe, whether at school, in the office or factory, on the roads or even at home. Factories often have a Safety Officer who has to make sure that everyone acts sensibly, and know what to do if there's a fire or emergency. Schools have rules that have to be obeyed, otherwise someone could be badly hurt. On the roads we have to follow the Highway Code, because roads are especially dangerous. Drivers have to keep to the left and stop at red traffic lights; cyclists must give proper hand signals and not ride two abreast: pedestrians are expected to stay on pavements and before they cross a road to check that no cars are coming. There are road signs to tell us what to do and warn us of danger ahead, speed limits to stop us going too fast, and other rules and regulations to keep us safe when travelling.

Some places are more dangerous than others. Machinery in a factory is usually far more dangerous than typewriters and filing cabinets in an office; the kitchen has sharp knives and other appliances more likely to cause an accident than anything in your bedroom. We take care to be safe, but we also like to feel safe too. The greatest danger comes is that when we feel safe and we don't take enough care. That's why so many accidents take place in the home. Danger is there whether or not we feel safe.

The Israelites weren't safe, because at the time Jeremiah was giving them God's message, the Babylonians had taken over from the Assyrians as the great superpower threat. Jeremiah had been told by God that they would be taken into captivity there from Jerusalem because of their disregard for God's laws and ways. They didn't believe him, at least not until what he said came true. Instead they tried to kill him, and stop him saying such things. Jeremiah had also been told by God that in time, he would make his people truly safe. They'd need to be saved first, of course, but he was going to deal with that too. They'd be saved by a coming King, who would not only bring them from captivity into freedom, but would give them a safe place to live. God often said his people were like sheep, and called those responsible for them shepherds. They hadn't done their job properly, so he was promising them new and caring shepherds to protect them; perhaps this passage reminds you of Jesus, the Good Shepherd (John 10). When we're guided and led by the Good Shepherd, we don't need to be afraid, because not only does he protect us from evil, he's actually defeated it by dying for us! We still have to take care crossing the road, and we must obey the rules which help keep everyone safe from accidents, but we can be sure that our God is looking after us, because he loves us so much, and nothing can happen to us without his hand being beneath us, and he will give us enough strength if we ask him.

Prayer
Thank you, Lord Jesus,
for your promise to keep us safe,
and to protect us.
We ask you to be our Good Shepherd
and guide us right through our lives.
Amen.

For Younger Children: Join together in designing a safety poster for your home – electrical appliances, gas cookers, smoke detectors, stairs, loose carpet . . . the scope is endless! Stress the importance of taking sensible precautions, but explain that whatever happens, God will keeps us in his care.

To Discuss: Has Jesus ever kept you safe from accident or danger, or do you know anyone who says he's protected them?

Thursday: Not An Alien

Reading: Zechariah 2:10-13

Not much longer to wait! By now I'm really looking forward to Christmas, and in a spare moment you might well find me looking through the programme listings to see if there are any good films over the holiday period. It's very frustrating to miss the film I most want to watch! Some really good films keep coming back, because they're so popular. Either they're hilariously funny or they've got a message behind the storyline which makes us think more deeply about our life: *A Passage to India* made me aware of the subtle dangers of racism, and the way we view people from other races and cultures. Perhaps you enjoyed *E.T.*, the story of the alien who comes to earth but only finds one person to befriend him. He looked so funny he couldn't pretend to be human, but in the way he was treated we can see a reflection of how we behave towards those who seem a bit different.

Jesus didn't, pretend to be human either, because he really was a man, who lived as we do and shared our life in every respect. But he *was* different, and as a result he was killed as a criminal, though he'd done no wrong. What made him different was his relationship with God his heavenly Father, who he listened to and obeyed right through his life. As he did his Father's will, it was as though he held up a mirror to the people of his day, so that they could see themselves properly. Some of them didn't like it at all and so they tried to get rid of him again and again until the opportunity came. They never realised that in Jesus, God was fulfilling his promise through Zechariah that one day he would come to live among his people. How sad! They wanted to keep God in heaven, far away and remote. God isn't like that: he doesn't stay up in heaven, looking down occasionally to see how we're getting on. He came to us in the person of Jesus to share our life and do all that was necessary to bring us back to our heavenly Father. He knows the temptations and difficulties we face, and longs to give us the forgiveness and freedom. God kept his promise – he did come to live among his people. He still does, by the power of his Holy Spirit, because although Jesus has ascended into heaven to be with his Father, he's still with us now, living in the hearts and lives of all who put their trust in him.

> **Prayer**
> Lord Jesus, you came to show us
> that you aren't a remote, far away God
> who doesn't care,
> but that you want to be
> in the very centre of our lives.
> We ask you to be our King
> and to help us trust you in everything.
> **Amen.**

For Younger Children: Discuss the feeling of being an outsider. Use a film or story from which you can draw a simple message for real life. Emphasise that the story of Jesus is real, as opposed to a fairy story, but from it we learn how God brought new life to us.

To Discuss: What will it mean for you today that Jesus is living within you?

Friday: Small Is Beautiful

Reading: Micah 5:1-5

Do you prefer things large or small? I used to think the best presents were the biggest ones, the ones that hardly fitted under the tree, but I know now that isn't always true. One Christmas my grandmother gave me a small package that didn't seem too interesting, so I left it for a while to open some other parcels. When I finally got round to unwrapping it, I found inside a beautiful wristwatch. It was a very special present, because soon afterwards she died. I can't even remember what else I received, but I still keep that watch. Sometimes the smallest things can turn out to be the best.

Perhaps you like other things that are small. We aren't fond of big cities, and much prefer smaller towns. They may not have so many shops and entertainments, but we enjoy them in a quite different way. Big places always seem more important and imposing. Governments are always found in a big city; a cathedral is huge in comparison with a small country church, because it's more important.

All of Israel expected God to do something to save them, and because he was God they assumed he'd do something big, in an important place so that everyone could see. God doesn't think like we do, however, so he sent his Son as a tiny baby born in an animal's feeding trough in a minor provincial town. He grew up in a carpenter's home in another small town, far from all the important places. He received no special education, and at the age of 30, when his ministry started, he had no permanent home. His friends were ordinary fishermen and tax-collectors, people who had little or no influence. When he died he was crucified as a criminal on Jerusalem's rubbish tip, and he was buried in a borrowed tomb. His resurrection was seen only by those whose eyes were open to what God was doing. Micah's message identified Bethlehem as the where God's salvation would be revealed to everyone, but people didn't realise that what we consider big and important may be nothing of the sort to God.

The whole of Jesus' life and ministry, his death and resurrection was rooted in the ordinary parts of life.

Best of all, God still uses people and situations that are ordinary to bring about his purposes. We may feel small and insignificant, unable to do anything useful for him. But he can't use people who are full of their own importance and cleverness, because they think they can do it all themselves. God uses those who ask for his help and strength, knowing their own weakness and failings. We'll never do anything for him in our own strength, but as we recognise how small we are compared to him, his Holy Spirit will take our smallness and make of it something beautiful for God's glory.

> **Prayer**
> Lord Jesus, we often feel
> small and helpless
> and thank you that that's how
> you came to our world.
> Please take our weakness and inadequacy,
> and by your Holy Spirit
> use them for your glory
> **Amen.**

For Younger Children: If you haven't done so already, why not have a present wrapping session? The point can also be made using something small and valuable like a watch or ring and a large, hideous vase, or similar white elephant! Explain that however 'small' we feel in terms of ability or opportunity, we're very precious to God, and He can use us just as we are.

To Discuss: How can we keep a balance between recognising and using the gifts we've been given by God, and thinking we can do things in our own strength?

Christmas

IN THE Western Church Christmas replaced the festivals surrounding the shortest day of the year. People feared that the sun, having gone down, wouldn't return, so they tried to persuade it to reappear by hanging evergreen foliage around their houses. It was Pope Julius I who established the date of Christmas in the West in AD 350, and from that time the Church incorporated some of the earlier traditions. Holly, for example, was a long-standing symbol of new life which acquired all manner of new meanings when associated with the birth and death of Jesus.

The Church's celebration of the birth of Christ may seem to us overshadowed by food and presents and other festive behaviour, but traditionally both have featured largely in Christmas celebrations. In Northern Europe especially, there is a tradition of baking cakes and biscuits in the shape of the infant Jesus, or of a star, or even of animals. The mince pie was originally pastry shaped like a manger into which spiced meats were placed. A figure of Christ made from dough was then laid in it. The Puritans regarded this as an abomination and although the custom re-started later, its symbolism was lost. Nowadays we find little echo in our present-swapping of God's supreme gift, which it represents, but there's little reason why these traditions of gifts, food and decoration shouldn't be reclaimed as a way of emphasising the Christian meaning of Christmas.

It's a pity that in emphasising the spiritual dimension of celebrating the birth of Jesus the Church has often (intentionally or otherwise!) been perceived as a kill-joy, looking to spoil everyone's fun. The best way to emphasise its spiritual significance is to celebrate it to the full and demonstrate the joy and happiness that Jesus brought into our world to all who accept and follow him.

The Christmas Tree

TREES have long been associated with the Christian celebration of Christmas. The Jesse Tree was a mediaeval device to show the genealogy of Christ in a tree form. It can still be seen in stained glass windows, carvings, and even candelabra, in some churches.

The teaching function of the Jesse Tree can be combined with the Christmas tree to help highlight the Christian significance of the Christmas festival. There is a story that St Boniface, the English Christian who went to evangelise Germany, once rescued a child from being sacrificed to the God Odin beneath a tree. As he explained to them about the story of Jesus he noticed a small fir growing there, and used it as a simple visual aid, saying that its evergreen leaves symbolised eternal life. He called it the 'Tree of the Christ Child'. Martin Luther once returned home from a walk in the starlight with a small fir-tree and decorated it with candles to remind his children that Jesus had left the glory of Heaven to come to our world as one of us. Trees and foliage had been used in pre-Christian times but soon became accepted as Christian symbols, though the Christmas tree was only introduced to Britain by Prince Albert, who was familiar with them from his childhood in Saxony, in the nineteenth century. You could use Luther's ideas and make some stars of card wrapped in silver foil to hang on your tree. Other symbols can also be used, and maybe you could make use of last year's Christmas cards to find some. Mary, for example, is often represented by a lily or a rose, and Joseph's carpenter's shop would provide some ideas to symbolise him. Jesus could be represented by a fish or a larger star, and it would be appropriate to include a Cross somewhere. Small gifts could bring home to us God's free gift of his Son, while some red ribbon might well stand for Jesus' blood shed for all of us. The Christmas tree can become a wonderful living symbol of all that the coming of Jesus means for us today.

Christmas Eve: The Happiest Event

Reading: Luke 2:8-14

What makes you really happy? Receiving the present you most want for Christmas, enjoying a family get-together, or something else? As we grow older we develop rather different ideas of what might make us happy and contented. For many couples that means having a baby of their own. When it arrives they call it a 'happy event'. It depends on what you mean by 'happy', of course. If it's one of those children who scream all night, Mum and Dad may miss their sleep; and not every big brother or sister is overjoyed about a noisy little bundle that takes up all their parents' time and energy. But everyone is happy that the baby has arrived safely and well. Mary and Joseph must have been delighted that Jesus was with them at last, healthy and fit, even if Augustus' census and the accommodation weren't quite what they had in mind! Their tiredness and irritation were transformed on that night Jesus was born.

The shepherds out in the fields weren't too happy. Shepherds were always viewed with distrust by 'nice' people, who thought of them as unreliable and dishonest. They usually kept to themselves, out with their flocks. Certainly the arrival of a baby down in the town wasn't something that would normally have interest. After all, no-one was interested in *them*, so why should it make any difference?

The happiness that night came from heaven. A choir of angels brought good news that night about the happiest event of all time. All heaven rejoiced, because despite the circumstances God had entered fully and decisively into human history, to bring his peace to a desperately needy world, and open the way for everyone to be able to enter his Kingdom. Nobody's excluded – even the shepherds, whom everyone ignored, were affected. They were the very first to be aware of what was happening, before all the important people. Best of all, the happiness of that night would last for ever.

We can enjoy being happy for a while, but the things we think will bring us happiness don't last for ever. We say, 'All good things come to an end'. The happiness Jesus brings will stay with us throughout our lives until we get to heaven, because it's based on the things we need most, forgiveness, new life, and hope. Jesus' birth was far and away the happiest event of all time!

Prayer for Christmas Eve

God our Father, we listen again to the story of Christmas, and we are glad that Jesus has come to be our saviour and our friend.

We hear how Mary laid her baby in a manger.
Jesus has come:
thank you, Father.

We hear how the angels sang over the Bethlehem hills: 'Glory to God; peace for the world.' Jesus has come:
thank you, Father.

We hear how the shepherds hurried to see that what the angel said was true. Jesus has come:
thank you, Father.

We hear how the wise men came to bring their worship and their precious gifts. Jesus has come:
thank you, Father.

O God, we thank you that Jesus has come to be our saviour and our friend: we welcome him with love, and worship him with gladness, for your glory's sake.
Amen.

For Younger Children: To make everyone happy, decorate the house with balloons; when they're inflated, write a 'happy' Christmas verse on them, such as 'Jesus – God with us' or 'Good news for everyone'. Make sure they're prominently displayed!

To Discuss: How can we share with our families and friends the happiness that Jesus brings?

Christmas Day: Pause For Thought

Reading: Luke 2:15-20

Happy Christmas! I hope you're having a great day and enjoying yourselves. You're probably all very busy, because there's so much to do today – Mum's got to prepare the lunch and serve it up (or does Dad do it in your home?); there are family and friends to welcome, games to play, presents to unwrap and find a home for! I hope you found time to go to church and worship God, too, and put Jesus right at the centre of his birthday celebrations.

Being busy can mean we don't have much time to think. So much is happening and everyone's talking or laughing, and we never really stop to work out what this is all about. Mary and Joseph weren't celebrating – at least, not with a party. They were too tired for that, and they still had the journey home to consider. In fact, very few people had even noticed their wonderful good news. So while Joseph looked after the practicalities, Mary sat with her new-born baby, watching him as he slept and waiting for the cry that told her he was hungry. The shepherds who'd come to visit were so excited they went off to tell the whole town, but Mary had no energy left. So she sat, and being a thoughtful sort of person she did some thinking. She knew all this was God's doing, that it was part of his great plan for the world, but as yet she couldn't quite grasp how. She let her mind wander over what all this meant, and I'm sure she realised one thing at least – that in her, on this night in a little provincial town, heaven and earth had met. Her tiny baby, only just arrived in the world, was also the God who had made that world, along with the stars and the universe. And this mighty God who she worshipped every day, had chosen her of all people to perform this astonishing miracle. Everything the angel Gabriel had told her was coming true. As the years went by, Mary must have wondered at the way God had worked in and through her, in order to bring forgiveness and new life to all who would accept it.

Like Mary, we may find it hard to see all that God was doing – it's beyond our ability to understand how the one who made everything and rules the whole universe could also become part of his own creation, weak and vulnerable, in order to put it right once and for all. Isaiah had foretold the coming of 'Emmanuel' – or 'God with us'. Now he'd really come, just as God had promised. He's still with us now, not as a tiny baby but as our king and saviour. That's worth thinking about not only today, but every day.

A Prayer for Christmas Day

Heavenly king, yet born of Mary;
Jesus Son of God,
we praise and adore you.

Eternal Word, yet child without speech;
Jesus, Son of God,
we praise and adore you.

Robed in glory, yet wrapped in infant clothes;
Jesus, Son of God,
we praise and adore you.

Lord of heaven and earth, yet laid in a manger;
Jesus, Son of God,
we praise and adore you.

To you, O Jesus,
strong in your weakness,
glorious in your humility,
mighty to save,
be all praise and glory,
with the Father and the Holy Spirit,
now and for ever.
Amen.

For Younger Children: If you have a crib, put Jesus in it, and at the same time light the fifth candle on the Advent Wreath. It's not the easiest day to encourage thought, but bring out the concept of God, who created the whole universe, becoming a tiny baby.

To Discuss: How will you make Jesus the centre of your celebrations this Christmas?

Boxing Day: Stephen's Witness

Reading: Acts 6:8-10, 7:54-8:1a

I hope you had a wonderful Christmas Day! The excitement of the Christmas holiday will continue for a few days yet, but we move on now from Jesus' actual birth, to a time of remembering that this was only the start of God's plan to bring us salvation and new life. In the Church's year, today isn't Boxing day but St Stephen's Day, when we think about Stephen and his witness to Jesus.

Some of the best dramas on TV include a courtroom scene, with somebody on trial and the jury having to announce a verdict. Will the innocent victim be acquitted of the crime he hasn't committed, or will the guilty party get away with it? It all depends on the witnesses. They're called to say honestly what they believe to be the truth, and on the basis of the evidence they give, the jury has to make up its mind about the case. Stephen was the first Christian martyr, but the Greek word from which we get our word martyr actually means a witness, someone who gives evidence. Stephen was killed because he bore witness to Jesus.

The religious authorities who wanted to kill Jesus never accepted that God his Father had raised him from death or that he was alive again. They saw him as an imposter, a wicked deceiver who had misled many people, and they certainly didn't want anyone saying he was still alive (or still worse, that his corpse had come back to life!) So what was the evidence that Jesus was the Son of God, the promised Messiah? The early Christians looked back at the whole of Jesus' life and ministry, his death and resurrection, and realised that only in him could everything make sense. All those prophecies in the Old Testament (some of which we looked at last week) came together in Jesus and revealed that he was the final part of God's plan; that he really was who he claimed to be; that God had now done everything he could possibly have done to save us and restore us to himself. Despite what had happened to Jesus, or rather because of it, they knew he was God made man, that all the events of the thirty-three years of his life made sense. More than that, they had a personal experience of him, and of God in him – they didn't just know *about* him, but knew him as their friend. No wonder they were prepared to face death rather than deny him and give up their new faith in him!

Jesus is easy to accept when he's only a tiny baby to be sentimental about, but more difficult when we encounter opposition to our faith. Amazingly, despite the cruel treatment of Christians over the centuries the Church still survives. The Church in Uganda has suffered more than most, and has seen many martyrs, yet it remains strong in its faith. Stephen, like all the early Christians, knew he had the power of the Holy Spirit within him, and because of that could stand firm against threats and ill-treatment. The same Holy Spirit has given strength to every Christian to stand firm when the going gets tough. Even if we aren't faced with that kind of opposition, we still need him to keep us loyal to Jesus and strong in our faith.

> **Prayer**
> Heavenly Father, thank you for all those
> who have faced suffering and death
> because of their witness to you.
> Please give us strength by the Holy Spirit
> to stand up for you whenever we're confronted
> with opposition, and keep our faith firm and sure.
> **Amen.**

For Younger Children: Older children might have fun enacting a courtroom scene. Perhaps someone could be on trial for stealing the Christmas pudding! Younger ones may find it easier to watch something happen, then describe exactly what they saw. Talk about what it means to be a witness, and how we can be witnesses for Jesus.

To Discuss: What is it about following Jesus that makes some people treat Christians so badly?

December 27th: John's Witness

Reading: 1 John 1:1-4

It's not good to tell lies. We all say things which aren't quite true, sometimes to get ourselves out of trouble, sometimes because we're showing off. It never pays – we end up telling another lie to cover the first one, and eventually we get found out. Most lies are fairly silly, but some are more serious. If you're a witness in court and tell lies, or try to prevent justice being done by giving false evidence, you're guilty of a serious crime. The law courts couldn't work unless they relied on people telling the truth.

Unlike Stephen, who we met yesterday, John wasn't killed for his faith, though he may have been imprisoned and persecuted for his witness to Jesus. He lived to a ripe old age and spent many years helping newly formed churches to understand and share their faith. We can't be sure whether he wrote his gospel before or after this letter, but in both he's at pains to point out that he's not writing fairy stories or adding imagination to history. He himself, with the other disciples, had seen and heard all that God the Father had done through his Son Jesus. More than that, John recognised that what he'd seen and heard was the source of new life, a life which goes on for ever for all who believe in Jesus.

At a time when many Christians were on trial for their faith, John wanted to reassure them that they weren't being killed and ill-treated for nothing. On the contrary, John, as an original eyewitness, could guarantee the authenticity of what was at stake. If what he'd written wasn't true, there would have been a lot of angry Christians accusing him of betraying them.

John wasn't only concerned with history, however. From his experience he knew that in recognising and believing the truth, Christians enter into eternal life, and are therefore joined together in Jesus. He calls it fellowship, a word we've used ever since, meaning something far deeper than mere friendship, or enjoying a common cause. Fellowship goes beyond all the barriers of race, culture, sex, colour and everything else that sets us against one another. It brings the joy that John wants his readers to experience – a new relationship with God through Jesus, and as a result, a new relationship with others.

John's witness to Jesus still remains in the Bible. Even if we don't write anything down, we too can share his love and joy with everyone. That really will last and the effects of that will also be lasting!

> **Prayer**
> Heavenly Father, please help us
> to share your love with others.
> Bring them the good news
> of your forgiveness and freedom
> which they too can share.
> May we be good and effective
> witnesses to everything we know
> and experience of you.
> **Amen.**

For Younger Children: If they can write, ask them to write down some facts about what happened on Christmas Day. If they can't, write it for them. You could also use a 'book of facts' such as an encyclopedia, to explain how everything needs to be checked for accuracy. Emphasise that the gospel writers were keen to write about what they knew was true.

To Discuss: If you were to write down an account of your faith, what things would you include?

December 28th: Lashing Out

Reading: Matthew 2:13-18

Christmas is a time for good news, so when bad news comes it always seems worse. The Lockerbie air disaster in 1989 was a terrible event by any standards, but coming as it did just before Christmas it seemed doubly tragic – many of those killed were on their way home to celebrate Christmas with their families. That event was very well publicised, but many people we never hear about also have a miserable time at Christmas, as a result of illness, bereavement, loneliness or anxiety. However much we enjoy our celebrations, we should never forget those who have nothing to celebrate.

Today's reading comes as a jolt after all the joy and praise and singing of the last few days. It's quite unpleasant in its way – we'd rather draw back from reading about a wicked king murdering a lot of baby boys. Herod was weak. Although he was called the king, in reality he was under the authority of the Roman Empire and had little personal power. Unfortunately he wouldn't admit it, and like most weak characters, the thought of a rival for his power frightened him silly. The last thing he wanted was another king in the land, and he certainly knew of the possibility of a Messiah sent by God. So to make sure he was safe he went on an orgy of destruction, lashing out in his fear and anger at all the eldest sons he could find. There were a lot of very unhappy families after that brutal and cruel behaviour. Jesus himself had to be rushed away into exile for a while until Herod had simmered down. He spent his earliest years as a refugee,

It may not be a pleasant reading, but we need an occasional reminder of the wicked and unkind way in which the defenceless and weak are sometimes treated. Herod was too much of a coward to deal with a genuine rival, but he was happy enough to kill little children unable to defend themselves. Jesus' coming to our world has a special significance for the weak and vulnerable. He had a particular mission to the poor and handicapped, the sick and suffering, the outcasts and rejects. He loved little children, and his attitude to women was revolutionary in its day. The gospels tell us time and again of Jesus' love and compassion for those in need, of how he took their side against those who exploited and ill-treated them.

Things haven't changed much in 2,000 years – there are still plenty of budding Herods around to abuse their power and take advantage of the weak. Following Jesus will sometimes bring us into conflict with the powerful, because it means that we too want to stand up for those in need. The Holy Spirit within us will enable us to share our own experience of Jesus' love with the downtrodden. In his strength we can help the helpless, befriend the friendless, protect the weak and speak out for the voiceless. Our contribution may seem very small, but the sea is made up of many tiny drops – if every Christian did something, what a difference there would be in the world!

Prayer
Heavenly Father, at this time of joy
help us not to forget or ignore
those who suffer.
Give us strength to do whatever we can
to help those who need
your love and compassion;
and show us what you want us to do
to make the world a better place
for everyone to live in.
Amen.

For Younger Children: This needs careful handling to avoid unnecessary fear or distress, but most children become aware that others are mistreated. Talk about caring for children, especially those in need. If your family has pets, you could start by discussing how to care for them, and then transpose some of those ideas to caring for people. Think of ways you could help children in need.

To Discuss: What practical action could you take this week to ease someone's suffering or deal with the cause of it?

December 29th: Light At Last

Reading: Luke 2:21-35

While I've been writing these words there's been some very strange news. I read in my newspaper that Britain is no longer an island, for the first time in 8,000 years apparently. Deep down, beneath the waves of the English Channel, well below the sea bed, English and French engineers have finally made contact. The two ends of the Channel Tunnel have now been linked in the middle, although the only sort of train you'd get through it at the moment would be a model one! Before long we'll be able to travel from London to Paris without getting on to a boat or off the train. We probably won't even catch sight of the sea! As tunnels go it'll be very long – a train travelling at sixty miles an hour would take just over twenty minutes to reach the other end (it sounds like the maths problems I used to do at school!) To walk to the other side would take at least a day. I can't imagine anyone wanting to, but if they did, I'll bet they'd be glad to see the first glimmer of light at the other end!

Simeon was an old man by now, and he'd been waiting all his life to see the glimmer of light that told him God was about to bring all his promises to fulfilment. As soon as Jesus was brought to him in the Temple by Mary and Joseph, he knew that this tiny baby boy was the promised Messiah, God's own Son, who he'd sent to bring light into the darkness of human history. Later on, Jesus called himself 'the Light of the World', because he came not only to the people of Israel in their misery, but to the whole world. Of all the hundreds of parents who came to Simeon with their babies, he knew that this child was the one he'd been looking forward to all his life. He was no different physically from any other boy, but God was at work in and through him, and he related uniquely to his Heavenly Father.

Whether the darkness is in ourselves or the world around us, it sometimes feels as though it will never end. Jesus the Light of the World comes to shine his light into the darkest corners of our life, the ones we try to avoid if we can. He can illuminate any darkness if he's allowed to shine there, and if at first that means clearing things up, then afterwards it looks and feels so much better. When we're in the dark, we stumble and bump into things, not sure where to go next. We need Jesus to help us see by his light. Once that light's shining, there's no more darkness. Just as Simeon recognised Jesus for who he was and saw the light he'd bring to the world, so can we come into that wonderful light and see our darkness completely dispelled.

Prayer
Lord Jesus, Light of the World,
shine into our hearts, we pray,
and drive away
darkness and sadness.
Help us to see by your light
your way for us,
and give us grace to walk in it
day by day.
Amen.

For Younger Children: Play a 'torch' game. You might switch it on in a dark room and have competition to see who can remember most what they saw in ten seconds. Explain how light removes darkness when it's switched on or allowed in, and how it removes fear of what's in the dark. Use the Advent Wreath candles to talk about Jesus, the Light of the World.

To Discuss: What sort of darkness does Jesus want to drive out today?

December 30th: A New Age Dawns

Reading: Luke 2:36-40

The old year's nearly over now. As you think back on all that's happened, what were the best and worst parts of it? Some years seem to have lots of good things to remember, while others have more than their fair share of bad. A 'new year' is only a way of helping us measure time, so that we can organise our lives and remember more easily when things occurred. Good and bad can happen at any time. Ten years ago, who would have predicted the downfall of so many Eastern European governments and their replacement with more democratic ones? And more recently, who could have foreseen the invasion of Kuwait in 1990, which led to the Gulf War? None of those events happened at the turn of a year, but for those affected by them life changed so much it will never be the same again. For the peoples of Eastern Europe there was freedom from brutal and tyrannical regimes as new authorities took over power, while for those in Kuwait, freedom from the invaders was realised when the allied armies marched in. Not that everything then became perfect, but the real change took place at that point in time.

It's easy to forget that 2,000 years ago those living in Palestine were ruled by a harsh government in far-off Rome and dominated by fear and poverty. Without much hope, they'd been looking forward for centuries to the coming of the Messiah, the new king who would restore the prosperity and happiness of King David's reign. But no-one thought to look for him in an ordinary inn, with ordinary parents, far away from kings and governments. At least, hardly anyone did. Yesterday we saw how Simeon recognised Jesus as the promised 'Light of the World'. Today we meet Anna, a very elderly lady who'd spent a great deal of her life with God in prayer. In the Temple when Mary and Joseph brought Jesus for the purification rite, she also realised that however ordinary his circumstances, this was no ordinary child. Her long relationship with God made her aware that a whole new spiritual dimension had entered the world. So she tells the other worshippers with the quiet joy of an old lady, that the redeemer was coming who would set God's people free – in fact, he'd already come.

It meant the dawn of a new era: an end, not to the tyranny of the Roman authorities, but to fear, despair, misery, and hopelessness. Jesus came to bring God's new Kingdom of light, peace, justice and joy to a world sadly lacking in many of those things. For the nations in Eastern Europe a new age dawned at the end of 1989 – they still have problems, but the chance to deal with them is there. God's Kingdom is quite different, to any human government, because Jesus has finally sorted out the problems of evil and suffering. To all who accept his authority, he still brings the forgiveness, peace and happiness we all long for.

Prayer
Heavenly Father,
thank you that we can be part of
your everlasting Kingdom through
Jesus' death and resurrection.
Please help us to do whatever we can
to bring its peace and justice
to the world.
Amen.

For Younger Children: Talk about different countries in the world and how they're governed. Explain how Christian people can make a difference to the things that happen in the world.

To Discuss: Many of the revolutions in Eastern Europe were strongly influenced by the Church and Christian people. Why do you think this was?

December 31st: Two Kingdoms

Reading: John 1:1-14 24:37-44

There's an American short story which tells of a man who went out to work one day in a thick mist. Although he didn't have far to go, the mist was so thick that he soon had no idea where he was. He walked on, enveloped in silence, until all of a sudden, he heard a faint beating sound. It became rapidly louder, until out of the gloom a large black crow flew straight at him! Can you imagine his terror? He ducked to the ground, his heart pounding. The crow for its part uttered at the same time the most appalling shriek of terror and squawked off as frightened as the man. He found his workplace and later on wondered why the bird had been so afraid. He eventually concluded that the crow had misjudged how high it was flying because of the mist, and hadn't realised how near the ground was, assuming the treetops were somewhere below. When it saw the man, it must have thought he was walking on air. The crow felt his world had been invaded by someone who shouldn't have been there! The man felt roughly the same way for a moment!

In becoming a man, Jesus brought God's Kingdom down to our world. He's God's living Word, and in him we can see something of what God is like. Although Jesus was God he became one of us. No longer could we criticise God for being too remote and distant, out of touch with his creation. In sharing our humanity he made it possible for us to share in his Kingdom, because two worlds overlapped. Our sinfulness meant we couldn't be part of God's Kingdom; his righteousness and goodness made it impossible. In Jesus' coming to this world, through his death and resurrection, we can be forgiven and made good enough to enter God's Kingdom. We have, as John says in today's reading, 'power to become the children of God', members not just of his Kingdom but of his family! And we don't have to do anything to earn or deserve it.

The man and the crow only experienced a momentary encounter with each other's world. But Jesus opens up for us the door to eternal life. Once we become part of his Kingdom, it's for ever. It wasn't limited to the time Jesus was actually on earth, because God sends us the Holy Spirit to be his power and presence. Instead of seeing and experiencing only our own world, he opens our eyes to God's Kingdom, and all that God is doing. Above all he gives us the blessings of being God's children, and the desire to share those blessings with others.

Prayer
Lord God, you came to show us
what you're like, and enable us
to become your children.
Please help us to live as members
of your eternal Kingdom.
Amen.

For Younger Children: Get everyone to draw heaven as they think it will be. Contrast this life with the next, and explain how Jesus was loved in this world, so that we could live in God's kingdom for ever.

To Discuss: How does being a member of God's Kingdom affect the way we live here and now?

January 1st: Claim Your Inheritance

Reading: Galatians 4:4-7

Happy New Year! Did you stay up to welcome it in, or take an early night to recover from all the excitement of Christmas? Whichever you did, today you can get out your new diaries and plan your year – if you know what's going to happen! The cheque book owners among you will need to remember to write in a different year, too – that's something I usually don't get used to until February! A new year doesn't make any real changes, of course If you had a streaming cold on New Year's Eve, you won't make a miraculous recovery when the clock strikes twelve. Even so, the new year is always as the opportunity to make a fresh start; to put the past year behind and turn over to a clean page.

Jesus' coming to our world wasn't like the new year arriving. The difference he made was far more important than just giving us a chance to make a fresh start. Many of our new beginnings fizzle out after a while – all those new year resolutions seem to be forgotten by Easter. Because of Jesus' death and resurrection we can enjoy new life as his children. That's a new relationship as well as a new start. And God's children, like any other children have rights. Children usually share their parents' home and have access to their resources. Later on, when the parents die, the inheritance that they leave behind becomes the children's property. We too have free access to our heavenly Father at any time, and all his resources are there for us to draw on as we serve him. He calls us his children because he wants us to know and love him as our heavenly Father. Paul wanted the Galatian Christians to realise that as God's children they had been given his Holy Spirit to reassure them of their freedom and their inheritance. Unfortunately they didn't let this affect their lives a great deal: it hadn't really made any difference. An inheritance is no use if the person to whom it is given it doesn't claim it or make any use of it. Jesus' coming to our world changes the lives of everyone who becomes a child of God, but we have to receive him first, or our inheritance will be useless. The Holy Spirit, God's living presence with us day by day, will transform us whatever time of year it is, but New Year's Day is a good time to make a fresh start with Jesus – a resolution that will last forever!

> **Prayer**
> Heavenly Father, thank you
> for your goodness in the past year.
> We commit ourselves to you
> for the whole of this coming year,
> to live as your children
> and receive all that you offer us
> through Jesus.
> **Amen.**

For Younger Children: Is there anything in your family inherited from an older generation? Any object will do, however mundane! Discuss how we inherit things from our parents, and how we can 'inherit' all that our heavenly Father wants us to have.

To Discuss: What sort of blessings might God have in store for you this year?

January 2nd: Happy Ever After

Reading: 1 John 2:24-28

Does your family have a special Christmas treat? One of the highlights of our Christmas has always been a family trip to the pantomime. It's so popular that we have to book our tickets in September! We love pantomime because it takes us away from our everyday lives to a fantasy world where wrong is put right and all's well that ends well. Whenever the villain appears, the audience boos and hisses. We love to hate Cinderella's wicked stepmother or Bluebeard the Pirate, and when he's beaten and made a fool of by the 'goodies' everyone cheers and stamps. In the end the hero and heroine get married and everyone lives happily ever after. We enjoy it because it's an escape for two hours to an ideal world, but we know that the real world isn't quite like that.

It would be lovely to think that this new year will be happy right through, but we can be fairly certain that some things won't go as planned. And to be quite honest, we're not too sure what 'happiness' is. A millionaire who was once asked what would make him a happy man replied, 'Just a little more money'. We may think that earning lots of money would make us happy, but if we did we'd probably feel no happier. Getting married sounds like a way to be happy, but people who are unhappy before they're married will very likely stay that way afterwards. The things that we think make us happy do no more than give us temporary enjoyment. There's nothing wrong with that, but it doesn't last very long.

In his letter, John tells his readers that there's only one way to be happy and stay happy – to 'remain in Christ'. Being a Christian isn't something we can do once, to see if we like it, and give up later if it gets too hard. Once we've started out on the Christian life we have to keep it up, but as we do we discover more and more that it brings real, lasting happiness. It isn't based on something that will soon be gone like money or a party, but on staying 'in Jesus'.

That means allowing him to rule our lives and show us the way he wants us to go. Our happiness as Christians is based on on life for ever with Jesus in his Kingdom. John calls it 'eternal life' and God has promised it to everyone who remains 'in Jesus'. There have always been plenty of people to distract us from things that last and keep us from following Jesus. They promise us real happiness now. John knew that his readers would hear similar voices telling them other ways to find happiness. But they'd never find any that lasts forever, except in Jesus. We don't have to try to 'remain in Christ': God's Holy Spirit reigning in our lives will give us the strength to say 'no' to everyone except Jesus.

Prayer
Thank you, Heavenly Father,
for the enjoyment we've had
during this Christmas.
Please help us to seek happiness
only by 'remaining in you',
and not letting other things distract us
from following you.
Amen.

For Younger Children: If you've been to a pantomime the difference between the story and reality is easy enough to draw out, although a good fairy story is equally helpful for this. Explain how Jesus helps us through the difficult times and knows about the reality of life, because he's shared it with us.

To Discuss: How does 'remaining in Jesus' help us through the unhappy times?

January 3rd: Just Like Father

Reading: 1 John 2:29-36

Have you seen any brand new babies recently? One of the strangest things about a baby's arrival is the way that its family and friends immediately start to say things like, 'He's just like his Father', or 'She's got her Mum's nose'. I sometimes wonder if I need spectacles, because I can't often see the likeness. Much of it's wishful thinking. After all, if you look at pictures of someone as they grow up you can see that they change beyond all recognition. There's a great party game in which everyone brings photographs of themselves as children and you have to identify who's picture is who's. But we don't just see similarities between people's faces or bodies. As a child grows up it develops its own personality and we begin to see that it shares some of its parents' characteristics in the way it behaves or speaks, reacts to situations, and even adopts the same attitudes. In fact, even if we don't look like our mother or father, there's almost certain to be at least one point at which we're similar to them.

Right through his letter John calls us 'God's children', and that's one of the things that makes us different as Christians. There's a family likeness which can be identified from the way we behave and speak, from our reactions and attitudes. As we grow up in the presence of our loving Father we become more like him, so that we can be seen increasingly as part of his family. We're not fully like him, and on this earth we never will be. Nor do we know exactly what we're becoming, but we can be sure it'll be much, much better than now, and we're looking forward to that time. In the meanwhile we can prepare ourselves for it.

The closer we get to God, however, the more we realise how sinful we are, how unworthy to come into his presence. We can never do anything remotely good enough to earn our way to his Kingdom. Jesus was good enough, could do enough, and was the only person ever who reached that standard. As result our sins are forgiven and we too are good enough to come before God. That's how we become his children and start to become more like him as we grow up in his love and his ways. Once we've set out on our Christian journey that process starts and it won't be long before people can see that there's a family likeness, and recognise our Heavenly Father in us.

> **Prayer**
> Heavenly Father,
> we don't deserve to be your children.
> Thank you that Jesus died
> so that we could be forgiven
> and become part of your family.
> May other people be able to see from our
> lives that you're our Father in heaven.
> **Amen.**

For Younger Children: Using photographs if necessary talk about how children take after their parents. Personality traits are also handed down from parent to child, and can be more revealing than physical ones! Stress that the people around us should know who our Father is, by the way we live.

To Discuss: What parts of our life could be identified by someone else as belonging to our Heavenly Father?

January 4th: Love Story

Reading: 1 John 3:7-10

How do you react when you watch a really sloppy romantic film? I mean the sort where the couple fall in love in the middle of all manner of disasters and tragedies, or never quite make it to the altar. Some folk pretend to be quite unmoved and unconcerned: 'it's only a story' they say. Others bawl their eyes out and end up with a wet hankerchief. Not all love stories are like that. Some are funny, others have a happy ending and a few are based on real life events. When we talk about a 'love story', what we often mean is a story about 'falling in love', which isn't quite the same thing. Being in love and staying in love, as most married couples soon discover, takes a lifetime's hard work, but they still need to fall in love first.

It's all very well telling someone how much you love them, whether it's your mother, your father, your husband or wife, your children, or someone else. Do you think they'll take you seriously if you don't behave in a loving way towards them? If you act as though you couldn't care less about them they'll soon come to the conclusion that you don't mean what you say. 'Actions speak louder than words' is a well-known saying. Why should anyone believe we love them if we speak rudely or unkindly, or treat them as though they're unimportant? Parents show they love their children by helping and protecting them; children show their love for their parents by obeying them; husbands and wives show their love by giving one another 'I love you' presents, and putting their interests aside for each other.

In today's reading, John tells his readers that if they say they love God, they must also act as though they do. We can demonstrate our love for Jesus by caring about other people as he did. If we treat them badly, exploiting them or treating them selfishly and unkindly, we can't love them very much. Nor can we love God too much. If we tell others that we love God, then we'll want to please him in our lives, to act as Jesus did, to show his love and compassion and mercy to those in need. That includes the ones we find it difficult to get along with, as well as those we like. It takes in the ones who usually get forgotten – the homeless, the elderly, the starving, the unemployed and the drug addicts. All of them were made by God, and desperately need to see his love demonstrated. The greatest love story of all was that Jesus gave up his life for all of us. His love spread out to everyone, even a common criminal who was crucified alongside him. If we mean what we say, then our love for God will be seen in the indiscriminate way we share his love with others.

Prayer
Lord Jesus,
we love you and praise you
for all you did for us.
Help us to show
we mean what we say
by sharing your love
with everyone we meet,
whoever they are.
Amen.

For Younger Children: Discuss how we know God loves us, and how people can see we mean it when we say we love God. How can we show we love another in a practical way? If you know someone in need of love, go as a family to show them Jesus' love in a way that helps them where they need it.

To Discuss: Who can we demonstrate God's love to today?

January 5th: You Need Only Ask

Reading: Matthew 24:37-44

I'm never sure whether I prefer presents which are a complete surprise, or ones that I've asked for in advance. It sometimes seems a bit rude to ask, but the trouble with surprise presents is that you can't be certain you'll get what you'd really like. The better I know the person giving the present, the more likely I am to ask them for something specific. There are occasions when asking is the right thing to do. I remember once as a boy feeling very offended that everyone else at the tea table was eating cake except me. I waited with a sulky face for someone to pass me the plate with the one remaining slice on it. 'What's the matter with you?' my mother asked. 'There's only one piece of cake left', I grumbled. 'Well?' she replied, 'what about it? You only have to ask for a piece. No-one's stopped you, have they?' I can't think why I hadn't asked, but I only had myself to blame that no-one knew I wanted a piece of cake.

Most children are quite willing to ask their parents for anything. But to have everything we want wouldn't be at all good for us: children who have whatever they want usually grow up selfish and spoiled. As God's children we can approach him to ask for anything. He won't fulfil our every desire like a magic genie, because he's a loving Father and knows that would do us no good. Instead he gives us the things we really need, sometimes without our even asking him! I'd love to have my own Jaguar car to drive, but to ask God for one would be selfish. The car I've now got isn't nearly as big, but it's comfortable and safe to drive and nowhere near as expensive to run. God has provided exactly what I need to do my job and transport my family. As we mature, we know what sort of requests our parents listen to or turn down. In the same way, growing as a Christian means we become more aware of the right things to ask God for. We learn to trust him to do exactly what's best for us, which may not be the same a what we'd like. Yet John tells us that we can come before God with complete confidence, if we're obeying him and doing what pleases him. Yesterday we saw how that means sharing his love with other people. As we serve God in that way, it changes the things we ask him for, so that instead of wanting an expensive car or bigger house, we ask him to help others in their need. If we're doing God's will, there's no doubt we'll receive answers to our prayers.

> **Prayer**
> Loving Father, we praise you
> for always being ready to hear us
> when we pray to you in faith.
> Please help us not to be selfish
> in our prayers but to ask,
> and trust you for the things
> which you know are best for us.
> **Amen.**

For Younger Children: Get them to ask for things, explaining how to ask properly. Help them to see that no-one can have everything they ask for, because they'd be very unhappy. Discuss what sort of things we can ask God for.

To Discuss: What sort of things should we be praying for?

Epiphany

EPIPHANY'S misfortune is to come at the end of the Christmas period, when going back to school or work, and removing decorations are at the top of the agenda. Originally the Eastern Church celebrated Christmas on this date, and only after East and West agreed to celebrate Jesus' birth together on December 25th did it become the festival of the visit of the Wise Men. In the West it has never included more than that, but other Christian traditions have widened the revelation of Jesus' true nature to incorporate his baptism, too. Many churches use the season of Epiphany (which continues until the Presentation of Christ, celebrated on February 2nd) to think about the Church's mission to the world.

As with Advent, there is scope for using the symbolism of light, especially with candles, and it's a good time to remember baptismal vows. But it's more than the end of the Christmas season. The weeks after Epiphany are used in the Alternative Service Book and other lectionaries to reflect on all that the incarnation implies and to link it more closely with Lent and Easter. Traditionally Epiphany, the 'Twelfth Night' after Christmas, is the time when the decorations and Christmas cards are taken down and put away. This is a job which really need doing by now: the tree is dropping its needles all over the floor, the holly is shrivelled and the cards are falling over and becoming a nuisance! Giving Epiphany a high profile enables us to build up the picture of Jesus' life and ministry, death and resurrection more fully and helps guard against the danger of putting Jesus away with the decorations until next Christmas.

Epiphany: The End Of The Beginning

Reading: Matthew 2:1-12

When I'm on holiday there are few things I enjoy more than reading an exciting detective novel. Some of my favourite television programmes are detective stories like *Inspector Morse* or *Sherlock Holmes*. I find I can't put the book down, or go and make a cup of tea, until I've seen how the problem works out. A good novelist or dramatist knows exactly how to throw in red herrings to distract us, and how to disguise the culprit until almost the very end. It takes us completely by surprise when his or her identity is revealed. What would you say to someone who put down their Agatha Christie after the third chapter because they didn't think there was any more to it, or switched off after twenty minutes of *Inspector Morse* because they thought it had finished? They couldn't possibly understand what was going on if they'd only seen more than the beginning. We can't form an opinion until we've seen the whole film, or read the book to the end.

Unfortunately there are a lot of people who think that Christmas is all there is to the story of Jesus. He stays as a tiny baby in a manger for them and they don't realise that they only know about the beginning. Today is called Epiphany because we remember how Jesus was revealed to the wise men, but more than that we can see too how in his coming to our world Jesus revealed His Father to us. Although we take our decorations and Christmas cards down today, and put them away until next Christmas, we can't do the same with Jesus. Even the gifts that those Eastern philosophers brought tell us of the rest of Jesus' life; the gold that speaks of his kingship, and his teaching about God's Kingdom; the frankincense that reminds us of his role as our great high priest praying for us; and the myrrh which takes us forward to his suffering and death for us on the Cross. The accounts of Jesus' birth make little sense, other than as a fairy story, unless we see the whole picture of his life, ministry, death, resurrection and ascension.

The wise men didn't come to admire a baby. They understood, if not fully, that there was much more to come, and that this child would become the centre of history. They worshipped him, because they had seen, however indistinctly, that this was the King of Kings. Epiphany marks the end of the beginning, but there's so much more to come! We can't put Jesus away, and if we allow him to be our king he'll stay with us throughout our lives by his Holy Spirit. He truly is Emmanuel, God with us for ever.

A Prayer for Epiphany

Christ, who was born in a stable,
give courage to all who are homeless:
in your mercy,
hear our prayer.

Christ, who fled into Egypt,
give comfort to all refugees:
in your mercy,
hear our prayer.

Christ, who fasted in the desert,
give relief to all who are starving:
in your mercy,
hear our prayer.

Christ, who hung in agony on the cross,
give strength to all who suffer:
in your mercy,
hear our prayer.

Christ, who died to save us,
give us your forgiveness:
in your mercy,
hear our prayer.

For Younger Children: Take a familiar story or film and see how important it is to know everything that happened, especially the end. Talk about the rest of the story of Jesus and how his birth was just the start of God's plan for the world.

To Discuss: Where, in our lives and our society, does Jesus still wait to be revealed?